Dress
Your Cake

Bake Them! Dress Them! Eat Them!

Dress Your Cake

Bake Them!   Dress Them!   Eat Them!

Joanna Farrow

spruce

An Hachette UK Company
First published in Great Britain in 2013 by Spruce
a division of Octopus Publishing Group Ltd
Endeavour House, 189 Shaftesbury Avenue,
London, WC2H 8JY
www.octopusbooks.co.uk
www.octopusbooksusa.com

Distributed in the US by Hachette Book Group USA
237 Park Avenue, New York NY 10017 USA

Distributed in Canada by Canadian Manda Group
165 Dufferin Street, Toronto, Ontario, Canada M6K 3H6

ISBN 978-1-84601-435-2
Printed and bound in China

10 9 8 7 6 5 4 3 2 1

This book includes dishes made with nuts and nut
derivatives. It is advisable for those with known allergic
reactions to nuts and nut derivatives and those who
may be potentially vulnerable to these allergies, such
as pregnant and nursing mothers, invalids, the elderly,
babies, and children, to avoid dishes made with nuts
and nut oils. It is also prudent to check the labels of
prepared ingredients for the possible inclusion of nut
derivatives. Some frostings include raw eggs. It is prudent
for the potentially vulnerable (as before) to avoid raw
or lightly cooked eggs. Small candies are suggested as
decoration. Care should be taken if used by or served
to small children. When using edible glitter and edible
gold or silver candies, ensure you use a product
labelled as "edible". Glitters described as "non-toxic"
are not the same as products labelled "edible" and
should not be eaten.

Publisher: Sarah Ford
Senior Editor: Sybella Stephens
Editorial Assistant: Ellie Sorell
Cover Design and Book Development: Eoghan O'Brien
Designer: Clare Barber
Photography: Lis Parsons
Food Styling: Joanna Farrow
Senior Production Manager: Peter Hunt

Glossary

- All-purpose flour = plain flour
- Baking cups = cupcake cases
- Chewy fruit rolls = fruit leathers and winders
- Confectioners' sugar = icing sugar
- Cookie sheet = baking tray/sheet
- Decorator frosting = writing icing
- Fondant sugar = fondant icing sugar
- Glucose syrup = liquid glucose
- Gummy candies = gums, gumdrops, wine gums, etc.
- Hard candies = boiled sweets
- Licorice laces = liquorice whips
- Light corn syrup = golden syrup
- Decorating tip = piping nozzle
- Plastic wrap = cling film
- Semisweet chocolate = plain chocolate
- Superfine sugar = caster sugar
- Turbinado sugar = light muscovado sugar

Contents

Baking Cakes

Birthdays, anniversaries, baby showers, seasonal celebrations, and any other big occasions are somehow made more special when there's an imaginative cake as the centerpiece. It commands attention among the other party food and, ultimately, every party guest tucks into it with relish. The inspiring cakes in this book are fun to make and pretty easy, too. All the equipment and ingredients are available from supermarkets and cake decorating retailers. If you've never made a party cake before, read the pages on basic techniques first so you're ready to go. A few of the recipes need time for icings to harden or set, so take a few minutes to read your chosen recipe and plan ahead. The cakes will keep well in an airtight container in a cool place for up to a week from baking to serving.

All the cake creations are made using the basic cake recipes on the following pages, though you can substitute a store-bought cake of any flavor in a similar size. However, the recipes on the next few pages couldn't be easier to bake and you will have the satisfaction of knowing that you've made the entire cake yourself. Ideally, bake the cake a day in advance so it has time to cool and firm up a little, particularly if it's being shaped before decorating. These cakes also freeze well.

Vanilla layer cake

This is a light, buttery, and moist sponge cake, perfect for stacking to make a taller cake by sandwiching the layers with buttercream and jam. You will need 2 pans to make this recipe.

Round cake pans	2 x 6 inch (15 cm)	2 x 7 inch (18 cm)	2 x 8 inch (20 cm)
Slightly salted butter, softened	⅔ cup /1¼ sticks (150 g)	1 cup/2 sticks (225 g)	1¼ cups/2½ sticks (300 g)
Superfine sugar	¾ cup (150 g)	1¼ cups (225 g)	1½ cups (330 g)
Eggs, beaten	2	4	5
Vanilla extract	2 teaspoons	1 tablespoon	4 teaspoons
Self-rising flour	1¼ cups (150 g)	1¾ cups (225 g)	2½ cups (300 g)
Milk	1 tablespoon	2 tablespoons	3 tablespoons
Baking time	25 minutes	30 minutes	40 minutes
SERVES	6–8	8–10	12–16

1. Preheat the oven to 350°F (180°C, Gas 4). Butter and line the required pans with nonstick parchment paper, then set aside. Using an electric hand or stand mixer, beat together the butter and sugar for 5–10 minutes, or until very pale and creamy.

2. Gradually add the beaten eggs, a little at a time. If the mixture starts to separate, stir in a tablespoon of the flour after each addition. Beat in the vanilla.

3. Sift the flour into the bowl and stir it in, adding the milk once the flour is almost combined. Divide the batter among the pans and level the surface with a spatula. Bake in the oven for the time stated above for the specific pan size, or until the surface feels just firm and a skewer inserted in the center comes out clean. Transfer to a wire rack to cool for a few minutes, then loosen the edges of the cakes with a knife and invert onto the wire rack to cool completely. Seal in plastic wrap and or store in an airtight container until ready to decorate.

Ingredients

- ⅔ cup/1¼ sticks (150 g) slightly salted butter, softened
- ¾ cup (150 g) superfine sugar
- 2 eggs
- 1 teaspoon vanilla extract
- 1 tablespoon milk
- 1½ cups (175 g) self-rising flour

MAKES 12

Vanilla cupcakes

For the cupcakes in this recipe, use the larger paper baking cups, which measure 4½ inches (11.5 cm) in diameter when flattened out. If you use smaller baking cups, you'll have batter left to make extra cakes. When adding the batter to the baking cups, do not fill them more than two-thirds full.

1. Preheat the oven to 350°F. (180°C, Gas 4) Line a 12-hole cupcake pan with large paper baking cups and set aside. Add the butter, sugar, eggs, vanilla, milk, and flour to a bowl and beat with an electric mixer until smooth and creamy. Divide the batter among the paper baking cups.

2. Bake for 25 minutes, or until risen, golden, and firm to the touch. Transfer to a wire rack to cool.

Variation

For chocolate cupcakes, make the cakes as above, replacing 3½ tablespoons of the flour with 3½ tablespoons unsweetened cocoa powder.

Rich chocolate cake

Even more moist and rich in chocolate than a regular chocolate cake, this recipe is perfect for any special birthday or celebration.

Round cake pan	6 inch (15 cm)	8 inch (20 cm)	9 inch (23 cm)
Square cake pan		7 inch (18 cm)	8 inch (20 cm)
All-purpose flour	1½ cups (175 g)	2¼ cups (275 g)	3 cups (350 g)
Unsweetened cocoa powder	3½ tablespoons	⅓ cup (40 g)	scant ½ cup (50 g)
Baking soda	1 teaspoon	1½ teaspoons	2 teaspoons
Light brown sugar, lightly packed	1 cup (200 g)	1½ cups (300 g)	2 cups (400 g)
Eggs	1	2	3
Milk or buttermilk	¼ cup (50 ml)	⅓ cup (75 ml)	scant ½ cup (100 ml)
Vanilla extract	1 teaspoon	2 teaspoons	1 tablespoon
Slightly salted butter	¾ stick (75 g)	½ cup/1 stick (100 g)	⅔ cup/1¼ sticks (150 g)
Unsweetened chocolate, chopped	3½ oz (100 g)	5 oz (150 g)	7 oz (200 g)
Water	½ cup (125 ml)	¾ cup (175 ml)	scant 1 cup (225 ml)
Baking time	50–60 minutes	1 hour	1¼ hours
SERVES	6–8	12–16	16–20

1. Preheat the oven to 350°F (180°C, Gas 4). Butter and line the required pan with nonstick parchment paper, then set aside. Add the flour, unsweetened cocoa powder, baking soda, and sugar to a bowl and stir to combine. In a separate large bowl, beat the egg(s), milk or buttermilk, and vanilla extract together.

2. Cut the butter into ½-inch cubes and add to a saucepan over low heat, then add the chocolate and water. Heat gently until the butter and chocolate have melted. (Do not let the mixture bubble up.)

3. Stir the dry ingredients into the egg mixture and add the melted chocolate mixture. Combine until you have a smooth batter. Pour into the pan and level the surface with a metal spatula. Bake for the time stated above for the specific pan size, or until firm to the touch and a skewer inserted into the center comes out just clean. Transfer to a wire rack to cool for a few minutes.

Madeira cake

This recipe makes a firmer sponge than a sandwich cake. It holds its shape well when baked in a pudding bowl and won't fall apart when cut into fun shapes.

Round pan	6 inch (15 cm)	7 inch (18 cm)	8 inch (20 cm)	9 inch (23 cm)
Square pan		6 inch (15 cm)	7 inch (18 cm)	8 inch (20 cm)
Slightly salted butter, softened	½ cup/1 stick (125 g)	¾ cup/1½ sticks (175 g)	1⅓ cups/2½ sticks (300 g)	2 cups/4 sticks (425 g)
Superfine sugar	⅔ cup (125 g)	1 cup (175 g)	1½ cups (300 g)	2¼ cups (425 g)
Eggs, beaten	2	3	5	7
Self-rising flour	1½ cups (175 g)	2¼ cups (250 g)	3⅓ cups (375 g)	4¼ cups (500 g)
Flavorings				
Lemons, zest grated	1	2	3½	5
Vanilla extract	1½ teaspoons	2 teaspoons	3½ teaspoons	1½ tablespoons
Baking time	45–50 minutes	55–60 minutes	65–70 minutes	1¼–1½ hours
SERVES	6–8	8–12	12–16	16–20

1. Preheat the oven to 325°F (160°C, Gas 3). Butter and the required pan with nonstick parchment paper, then set aside. Using an electric hand or stand mixer, beat together the butter and sugar for 5–10 minutes, or until very pale and creamy.

2. Gradually add the beaten eggs, a little at a time. If the mixture starts to separate, stir in 1 tablespoon of the flour after each addition. Beat in your chosen flavoring.

3. Sift the flour into the bowl and stir until combined. Pour the batter into the pan and level the surface with a metal spatula. Bake for the time stated above for the specific pan size, or until a skewer inserted into the center comes out clean. Transfer to a wire rack to cool.

Buttercream, Fondant, and Ganache

Here are all the toppings used to decorate the cakes in this book. You can make rolled fondant yourself, but it is available in grocery stores and online in a wide range of colors.

Ingredients

- ⅔ cup/1⅓ sticks (150 g) unsalted butter, softened
- 1¾ cups (225 g) confectioners' sugar
- 2 teaspoons vanilla extract
- 2 teaspoons boiling water

Vanilla buttercream

This is used for filling layer cakes, but can be spread on the top and sides, too. It is also used for piping decorations. It's easy to add food coloring to, and any leftover mixture will keep well in the refrigerator for a few days.

1. Add the butter, sugar, and vanilla extract to a bowl and beat with a wooden spoon until smooth.

2. Add the boiling water and beat again until pale, light, and fluffy.

Variations

For lemon buttercream, omit the vanilla and add the finely grated zest of 3 lemons. Then add 1 tablespoon lemon juice instead of the water.

For chocolate buttercream, beat in ⅓ cup (40 g) unsweetened cocoa powder and add an extra tablespoon of boiling water.

More frostings over the page...

Ingredients

- 1 medium egg white
- 1½ cups (225 g) confectioners' sugar

Royal icing

Royal icing sugar mix is available in some supermarkets and specialty cake decorating stores. Follow package directions for the amount of water to add to make the icing. It's equally easy to make your own using this recipe. You can use it instead of store-bought frosting tubes, with the advantage that you can make up any color and put it in a paper pastry bag (see page 20).

1. Put the egg white in a bowl and lightly beat to break it up. Add half the confectioners' sugar and beat until smooth.

2. Gradually work in the remaining confectioners' sugar until the icing has a thick, smooth consistency that just holds its shape. Cover the surface of the icing with plastic wrap until ready to use to stop a skin from forming.

Ingredients

- 1 medium egg white
- 2 tablespoons glucose syrup or light corn syrup
- About 4½ cups (250 g) confectioners' sugar

Homemade rolled fondant

This is an icing that's well worth buying readymade. Versatile and fun to use, rolled fondant can be rolled out like pie dough for covering cakes in a smooth layer or for molding into shapes for decoration. White and basic primary-colored rolled fondants are available from supermarkets, or for a wider range of colors, try specialist cake decorating stores or online suppliers. However, it is easy to work coloring into rolled fondant (see page 15).

1. Put the egg white, glucose or light corn syrup, and about a quarter of the confectioners' sugar in a bowl and mix to a smooth paste.

2. Continue to mix in more confectioners' sugar until it becomes too stiff to stir. Turn the paste out onto the work surface and knead in more confectioners' sugar to make a smooth, stiff paste. (If too soft and sticky, the fondant will be difficult to work with.)

3. Seal the fondant tightly in several thicknesses of plastic wrap until ready to use.

Dark chocolate ganache

Chocolate lovers will adore this smooth, creamy frosting. It can be used as a filling for layer cakes, and as a frosting, and it pipes well, too. Spread onto cakes when freshly made (but cooled) because it sets hard if stored in the fridge.

1. Put the chocolate in a bowl. Add the cream and sugar to a saucepan over medium heat and stir until the mixture bubbles up around the edges but is not boiling. Pour the cream mixture onto the chocolate and let stand, stirring frequently, until the chocolate has melted and the consistency is smooth and silky.

2. Let stand until the ganache is cool enough to hold its shape before using. (Chilling the ganache in the fridge will speed up cooling but keep an eye on it because it will eventually set.)

Variation

For white chocolate ganache, use the same quantities but omit the confectioners' sugar. Heat only half the cream to pour over the chocolate. Once the chocolate has melted, stir in the remaining cream and use as above.

Ingredients

- 10 oz (300 g) semisweet chocolate, chopped
- 1¼ cups (300 ml) heavy cream
- 3 tablespoons confectioners' sugar

General Decorating Techniques

If you haven't decorated a cake before, take a look at the following helpful techniques, which will set you on the path to achieving professional results.

Covering cakes with buttercream

1. Before covering a cake, trim off any excess dome if the cake has risen in the center during baking. However, do not slice off the entire dome to attempt to make the top the same level as the edge of the cake or the cake will be too shallow. Instead, start by slicing off the crust at a point that's halfway between the peak of the dome and the edge of the cake. Now invert the cake onto a board with the flat base uppermost. If there's still a huge gap between the bottom of the sides of the cake and the cake board, slice a little more of the dome off the top.

2. Split the cake in half and, using a spatula, spread a layer of buttercream (or jam if the recipe calls for it) onto the top surface of the bottom layer, and replace the top layer. Make sure you fill the gap between the cake board and the base of the cake with buttercream as well before covering the cake with rolled fondant.

Melting Chocolate

Melted chocolate is used for spreading and piping. Avoid overheating or you'll spoil its smooth texture.

To melt on the stove top: Break the chocolate into small pieces and put in a heatproof bowl. Set the bowl over a saucepan of gently simmering water, making sure the base of the bowl doesn't come in contact with the water. Once the chocolate starts to melt, turn off the heat and leave until completely melted, stirring once or twice until no lumps remain.

To melt in a microwave: Break the chocolate into chunks and put in a microwave-proof bowl. Let melt 1 minute at a time, checking frequently, until the chocolate is partially melted. Remove from the microwave and stir frequently until all the remaining chocolate has melted. Take care when melting white chocolate because it is more likely to burn due to the high sugar content.

Using rolled fondant

Before rolling or shaping fondant, dust a little confectioners' sugar onto the work surface. This stops the fondant from sticking. Rolled fondant dries out quickly, so any fondant that's not being worked with should be sealed in plastic wrap or its texture will spoil. If it does dry out on the surface because it hasn't been completely sealed, you can cut off and discard the edges and the center should still be soft and pliable.

Adding color

Liquid food colorings are generally acceptable for adding a pastel shade but for stronger colors, paste or gel food colorings are more effective. Dot the coloring onto the fondant with a toothpick and knead it in on a surface dusted with confectioners' sugar. Use the food coloring sparingly at first until you're sure of its strength—you can always blend in more if you want a richer color. If not using immediately, seal tightly in plastic wrap.

Blending colors

Basic primary colors can be kneaded together to create more unusual colors. Use the same principle as mixing paints: red and yellow can be mixed to make orange; blue and red to make purple; red and white to make pink; and black and white to make gray.

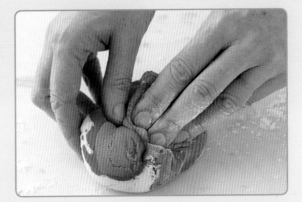

Rolling out fondant

In this book, fondant is generally rolled to two different thicknesses (unless a recipe states otherwise). For covering a cake it's rolled until slightly thicker than you would pie dough, about ¼ inch (5 mm). Where a recipe states "thinly roll" (usually for decorations, such as ribbons and flowers), the fondant should be about ¹⁄₁₆ inch (2 mm) thick or thinner. The thinner the fondant is rolled, the more delicate the finish will be.

Covering a cake with rolled fondant

1.

2.

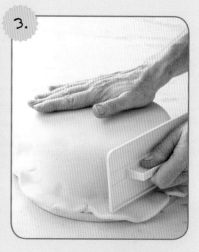

3.

Dust the work surface with confectioners' sugar and lightly knead the fondant to make it pliable. Roll out to a circle or square that's about 6 inches (15 cm) larger than the diameter of the cake. Keep lifting and turning the fondant, as you would pie dough, so it doesn't stick to the surface. Drape the rolled fondant over the cake.

Smooth the fondant over the top of the cake and around the sides, easing it to fit. Because rolled fondant is so pliable, you should be able to fit it around the sides without leaving any creases.

Trim off the excess around the base. Lightly dust your hands with confectioners' sugar and use the palms of your hands to smooth out any bumps. You can use an icing smoother (see above), to get a good flat surface.

Covering a cake board with rolled fondant

Dampen the cake board with a pastry brush moistened with water. Thinly roll out the fondant on a surface dusted with confectioners' sugar until slightly larger than the size of the board. Carefully transfer the fondant to the board so the ragged edges just overhang the rim of the board. Lightly dust your hands with confectioners' sugar and use your palms to smooth out the fondant, or you can use an icing smoother. Trim off the edges with a sharp knife and run your fingers around the edges to check they are completely smooth.

Covering the bare surface around the cake

Moisten a fine paintbrush and use it to dampen the cake board surrounding the cake. Thinly roll out the fondant on a surface dusted with confectioners' sugar. For a round cake, roll the fondant into a long strip, curving the icing as you roll. When it's large enough, cut the inner edge of the strip and position so the cut edge butts up against the cake. Smooth down the fondant, overlap the ends, and remove the excess. Smooth the join and trim the edges as above.

For a square cake board, moisten a fine paintbrush and use it to dampen the bare surface of the cake board as above. Thinly roll out the fondant to a strip slightly longer than the length of the board. Cut 4 strips and lay one along each side of the board around the cake, butting it up neatly against the side of the cake. Miter the corners where the strips overlap. Smooth out the joins and trim the edges as above.

Modeling rolled fondant

Modeling is fun to do and is very similar to molding modeling clay. Keep your hands lightly dusted with confectioners' sugar and make sure the fondant you're molding is smooth and not drying out in places. Use the required amount of fondant suggested in the recipe. Mold it until you're happy with the shape, using the photographs as a guide. Leave the shape to set on parchment paper or secure directly to the cake, as the recipe requires. Finish by painting or adding any further decorations.

Rolling shapes into fondant

Rolling contrasting colors of fondant together, but without blending in their colors, makes an easy and incredibly effective decoration. This method is used frequently in this book on cakes, such as the Chic Purse and Bunting Bonanza cakes. You'll need to work reasonably quickly with this technique so the fondants don't dry out before you've finished.

Thinly roll out the fondant on a surface dusted with confectioners' sugar. Break off tiny pieces of fondant in a contrasting color. Roll the tiny pieces into balls, strips, or whatever the recipes calls for, and arrange them on top of the rolled fondant.

Dust a rolling pin very lightly with confectioners' sugar and roll it two or three times over the two fondants, lifting the fondant after each roll so it doesn't stick to the surface. Cut out shapes as required.

Using fondant trimmings

It's vital that you keep any fondant you're not working with tightly sealed in plastic wrap, particularly in a warm kitchen, because it dries out quickly. Trimmings can be reworked repeatedly as long as they are not allowed to dry out, so after rolling and cutting out fondant shapes, gather up the trimmings, knead into a soft ball, and seal in plastic wrap. Once the cake is finished, any substantial amounts of fondant can be wrapped in several layers of plastic wrap and stored in an airtight container for use another time.

Securing fondant decorations in place

When rolled fondant is used to cover a cake that has been frosted with buttercream, the buttercream holds the fondant in place. When securing fondant to another layer of fondant, however, you'll need to very lightly brush the fondant first with a dampened paintbrush. Dip the brush in some cold water and then squeeze the bristles to remove any excess. If too much water is left on the brush, the fondant won't stay neatly in place and the texture of the fondant will be spoiled.

Cutting out and shaping plunger cutter flowers and leaves

Plunger cutters are simple to use and give the cake a professional finish. Roll out the fondant as thinly as you can on a surface dusted with confectioners' sugar. Cut out a flower or leaf shape with a plunger cutter and then, using the plunger attachment, push the shape out onto a piece of nonstick parchment paper. Alternativley, the flowers can be placed directly onto the cake by dampening the center of the flower with a paintbrush first and securing it in position. Flowers cut this way will set in a natural-looking shape, but leaf shapes are best left on crumpled parchment paper so they set in a curved shape.

Making and using templates

Several of the recipes in the book use templates (see pages 126–7). To use, trace the template onto paper and cut it out. Thinly roll out the fondant (unless the recipes states otherwise) and gently rest the template on top. Carefully cut around the template using the tip of a small sharp knife.

A couple of the recipes use the template as an outline shape for filling in. Trace the template onto paper but don't cut it out. Slide the paper under a sheet of parchment paper so the shape shows through. Pipe over the outline, then slide the template to a clear area of paper so you can pipe more.

Pastry Bags and Tips

Buttercream, royal icing, and melted chocolate are all suitable for piping. Reusable pastry bags in different materials can be bought readymade, but it is more economic, and so easy, to make your own. They can be fitted with a plain or star tip for piping, or simply used with the end snipped off.

How to make a paper pastry bag

Both parchment and wax paper can be used, though nonstick parchment paper is more durable. For filling and using piping bags, see opposite.

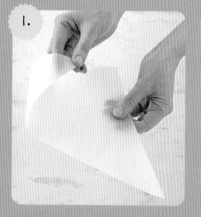  

1. Cut out a 10-inch (25-cm) square of nonstick parchment or wax paper. Fold it diagonally in half and then cut the paper in half just to one side of the fold. Take one triangle and hold it with the long edge facing away from you and holding the point nearest you with one hand.

2. Curl the right-hand point over to meet the center point, shaping into a cone.

3. Bring the left-hand point over the cone so the three points meet. Fold the points over several times so the cone shape is secured in place.

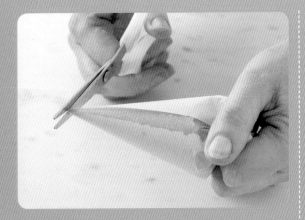

Filling a paper pastry bag fitted with a tip

Cut off about ¾ inch (2 cm) from the point and insert the tip. Half fill the bag with buttercream or royal icing and twist the open end to secure.

Filling a paper pastry bag without a tip

Use the same technique as above, but don't cut off the point of the bag before filling. Fill the bag and twist the open end to seal. Then snip a very small amount off the point, so the icing can be piped in a thin line, as called for in most recipes in this book. This is particularly important if you're piping an outline or fine detail. You can always snip off more of the point if the line is too thin.

Using chocolate for piping

Melted chocolate is best piped without fitting a tip because melted chocolate sets quickly. If the chocolate does set, you can soften it by placing the pastry bag very briefly in the microwave. Remember, you can't do this if using a metal pastry tip.

Softening butter

Most cake recipes require softened butter so it can be blended easily with other ingredients to make a smooth, creamy mixture. Even at room temperature butter can still be quite firm, so the best way to soften it quickly is to use the microwave. Cut the measured butter into small pieces in a bowl. Microwave on medium power in short bursts until the butter is soft enough to push your finger into it. Don't leave the butter in the microwave for too long or it will melt. For melting butter to grease pans, melt a little butter in the same way, but watch it closely or it will start to splutter if left too long.

Softening fruit chews

If you can squeeze a fruit chew between your fingers to flatten, it's probably soft enough to shape into a decoration. If it is brittle, heat it in the microwave first. Place the unwrapped chew on a piece of nonstick parchment paper and heat on full powder for 3–4 seconds. Once softened, mold the chew into the desired shape. Take care when softening a chew because it will melt very quickly and become scalding hot.

Securing ribbon around cake boards

For the final, finishing touch to your cake, you can wrap ½-inch (1 cm) wide colored ribbon around the cake board. Secure it at the back with a straight pin or double-sided adhesive tape. Choose a ribbon in a color that complements the colors used on the cake.

Useful Equipment

The recipes in this book list some pieces of equipment you might not already have in your kitchen. However, all are available from department stores, cake decorating outlets, or online suppliers.

Round and square cake pans

Pans with a fitted or loose bottom are suitable. Make sure they are deep sided so the cake batter doesn't spill over the top during baking.

Lining a round cake pan

Draw around the pan on a piece of nonstick parchment paper, cut out the circle, and set aside. Cut a strip of nonstick parchment paper that is slightly wider than the height of the pan and longer than the circumference. Fold a ¾-inch (1.5 cm) lip along one edge and snip the lip at intervals as far in as the fold. Brush the inside of the pan all over with melted butter. Fit the paper strip around the inside edge of the pan, allowing the snipped edge to sit on the bottom of the pan. Set the circle of paper into the bottom of the pan covering the snipped edge. Then grease the paper.

Lining a square cake pan

Use the same technique as for a round pan but only snipping the strip in four places to make the paper fit the 4 corners of the pan.

Lining a loaf pan

Cut out a wide strip of nonstick parchment paper that's long enough to cover the bottom and long sides of the pan and hang over the long sides slightly. Grease the inside of the pan all over and press the strip in place. Grease the paper. Once the cake is baked, you can loosen it at the ends of the pan with a knife and then lift the cake out by holding the ends of the overhanging paper.

Deep round cake pan

The madeira cake recipe (see page 10) requires a deep pan in which the sides are at least 1¾ inches (4 cm) so the batter doesn't spill over the top during baking.

Lining round cake pans using flour

Draw around one of the pans on a double-thickness piece of nonstick parchment paper and cut out two circles. Grease the pans and press the paper into the bases. Grease the papers. Tip a little flour into one side of the pan and tilt the pan so the flour adheres to the sides. Shake out the excess and repeat with the other pan.

Loaf pans

These are useful for making a deep-sided, rectangular shape.

Pudding bowls

Ovenproof glass, ceramic, silicone, or metal pudding bowls are used for making domed-shaped cakes.

Lining a pudding bowl

Grease all over the inside of the bowl. Cut a circle of nonstick parchment paper that's large enough to cover the base and come slightly up the sides of the bowl. Fold into a cone shape, make cuts ¾–1¼ inches (2–3 cm) from the curved side toward the point, open out, and use to line the bottom. Grease the paper.

Food cans

Thoroughly cleaned food cans with a capacity of 1lb 12oz (800 g) are used for baking some of the cakes. Grease and line the can as you would a cake pan.

Metal spatula

A small, flexible metal spatula is useful for spreading buttercream or chocolate ganache when you want a fairly smooth surface.

Plunger cutters

Available in an increasingly varied range of shapes and sizes, plunger cutters are great for cutting out and shaping flowers and leaves (see page 19).

Pastry bags

The recipes in this book are designed for using small pastry bags. You can color royal icing as you require and use it for piping decorative details. Store-bought tubes of decorator frostings make an easier alternative, though the colors are available in a more limited range.

Nonstick parchment paper

Used for lining pans and pudding bowls, making pastry bags, tracing templates, and as a surface for allowing shapes to harden on.

Cutters

These come in a wide range of shapes and sizes both for stamping out intricate shapes and larger, cookie-sized decorations.

Cake boards

Cake boards are about ½ inch (1 cm) in thickness, and are used in all the recipes as a secure base for your creations. Thin cake boards, sometimes called cake cards, can also be used, though they're not quite as effective.

Paintbrush

A fine paintbrush is ideal for painting food coloring onto frosting, for securing decorations in place, and for dampening cake boards before covering with rolled fondant.

Decorating tips

Decorating tips are available in many different shapes and sizes. For this book, you need "star" or "leaf" tips, which can be fitted into paper pastry bags with ½ inch (1 cm) cut off the pointed end. "Writer" tips are also available and can be used instead of tubes of decorator frosting or pastry bags with the very end of the point cut off.

Toothpicks

These are useful for adding tiny quantities of paste or gel food coloring to buttercream, royal icing, or rolled fondant.

Icing smoother

This is a flat plastic tool that's great for giving a perfectly smooth surface to rolled fondant.

Under the Sea

Ingredients

- 7-inch (18-cm) round vanilla layer cake (see page 7)
- ¼ cup (4 tablespoons) raspberry or strawberry jam
- Vanilla buttercream (see page 11)
- 9-inch (23-cm) round cake board
- 1½ lb (750 g) bright blue rolled fondant
- Confectioners' sugar, for dusting
- 3½ oz (100 g) pink rolled fondant
- Small piece yellow rolled fondant
- 3 oz (75 g) orange rolled fondant
- 1½ oz (40 g) white rolled fondant
- Royal icing (see page 12)
- Black food coloring
- ⅓ cup (50 g) turbinado sugar

Equipment

- Metal spatula
- Rolling pin
- Sharp knife
- Fine paintbrush
- Paper pastry bag (see page 20)
- Small round writing tip

Cover the cake: Halve the cake horizontally and sandwich the layers together with the jam and half the buttercream, then place on the board. Frost the top and sides with the remaining buttercream. Roll out the blue fondant on a surface dusted with confectioners' sugar and use to cover the cake (see page 16). Reroll the trimmings and use them to cover the surface of the board around the cake (see page 17).

Pink fish: Roll 2½ oz (65 g) of the pink fondant into an oval shape. Flatten it down slightly on the work surface and pinch in the top to shape the fish. Bend the shape slightly and secure on top of the cake with a dampened paintbrush. Use a little more pink fondant to shape a tail, fin, and curved lips, then secure in place. Thinly roll the yellow fondant, cut it into wavy strips, and secure them to the fish.

Crab: Take ⅓ oz (10 g) of orange fondant and roll it into a small ball. Then take 2 pea-sized pieces of orange fondant, roll them into little balls, and make a cut to the centers to shape pincers. Secure these to the base of the cake and set the larger ball on top of them to complete the crab's body.

Octopus: Reserve ½ oz (15g) of the white fondant. Knead the remainder with the rest of the pink and orange fondant to make a coral-colored fondant. Mold a ½-oz (15-g) piece into a pear shape for the octopus's head. Cut another ½ oz (15 g) into 8 pieces. Roll each under the palms of your hands for tentacles, tapering each to a point at one end. Secure in a circle to the top edge of the cake and push the head gently down in the center.

Sea plants: Add the royal icing to a paper pastry bag fitted with the writing tip (see page 21) and pipe coral shapes onto the sides of the cake. Flatten small pieces of coral-colored fondant and roll up between your fingers. Arrange in clusters around the base of the cake, securing them in place with the royal icing.

Finishing touches: Shape and position eyeballs for all the creatures using small balls of white fondant. Paint facial features and pupils for the eyes using black food coloring. Sprinkle plenty of turbinado sugar around the base of the cake. Pipe air bubbles around the sides and wave marks on top of the cake using the royal icing.

who else is enjoying a swim...?

Penguin Party

Ingredients

- 8-inch (20-cm) round vanilla layer cake (see page 7)
- 12-inch (30-cm) round cake board
- Vanilla buttercream (see page 11)
- 2 lb (1 kg) white rolled fondant
- Confectioners' sugar, for dusting
- 5 clear hard candies
- Royal icing (see page 12)
- Blue food coloring
- 3 oz (75 g) black rolled fondant
- Small piece orange rolled fondant
- 1 white candy stick
- Small piece red rolled fondant

Equipment

- Sharp knife
- Metal spatula
- Rolling pin
- Cookie sheet
- Parchment paper
- Fine paintbrush

Shape the cake: Cut a zigzag line through one cake layer, not quite through the center. Place the larger piece on the board. Cut the rest of the cake into irregular pieces, adding two further layers to the piece on the board to create three layers in all. Shape a separate section using two layers and a third of one layer to create irregular iceberg shapes. Fill the cake layers with half the buttercream, then frost the iceberg- shaped cakes with the remainder.

Icebergs: Roll out two-thirds of the white fondant on a surface dusted with confectioners' sugar. Drape the fondant over the cake. Fit it all around the sides, easing it in place and molding it into the corners. If necessary, patch up any uncovered areas with extra fondant. Trim off the excess around the base. Cover the remaining iceberg cakes with fondant. (You might find it easier to cover these on the work surface, then transfer them to the board.) Reserve the fondant trimmings.

Sea: Line a cookie sheet with parchment paper and preheat the oven to 400°F (200°C, Gas 6). Unwrap the candies and space them well apart on the paper. Place them in the oven for 5 minutes, or until the candies are melted and syrupy. Let cool on a wire rack. Spread the royal icing around the icebergs, making peaks with the metal spatula. Peel the paper away from the cooled candies and rub a little blue food coloring over the bases. Push down into the royal icing, snapping where necessary to fit, to create areas of sea.

Penguins: Roll a ⅓-oz (10-g) ball of white fondant and stretch it into an oval shape. Flatten two pea-sized pieces of black fondant between your fingers to shape wings and secure to the body with a dampened paintbrush. Roll and position a ball of black fondant for a head. Shape tiny pieces of orange fondant into feet and make several indents in each with the tip of a knife. Position the feet on the cake and press the penguin body on top. Roll and position tiny balls of white fondant for eyeballs. Mold a tiny diamond shape in orange fondant for a beak, pinch it in half, and secure it to the face.

Paint pupils on the eyes with blue food coloring. Repeat to make 6 more penguins. For a diving penguin, position a cherry-sized ball of white fondant on the "sea," secure a small flap of black fondant to one side of the ball, and add orange feet to the other.

Flag: Push the candy stick into the white fondant. Cut a triangle of red fondant and secure to the top of the flag with a dampened paintbrush.

Iceberg icing!

Toadstool Cottage

Ingredients

- 8-inch (20-cm) quantity vanilla Madeira cake batter (see page 10)
- 5 oz (150 g) green fondant
- Confectioners' sugar, for dusting
- 9-inch (23-cm) round cake board
- Vanilla buttercream (see page 11)
- 13 oz (400 g) white fondant
- 10 oz (300 g) red fondant
- 1 oz brown (25 g) (or chocolate-flavored) fondant
- 2 oz (50 g) each yellow and pink rolled fondant
- 1 small yellow candy
- Tube of green decorator frosting
- Selection of sugarcraft flowers

Equipment

- 6-inch (15-cm) round cake pan, lined with parchment paper (see page 22)
- 2-quart (2.5-litre) ovenproof pudding bowl, lined with parchment paper (see page 24)
- Pastry brush
- Rolling pin
- Sharp knife
- Metal spatula
- String
- 1¼-inch (4-cm) and 1¾-inch (3-cm) round cutters
- Fine paintbrush

Bake the cake: Add 1½ lb (750 g) of the cake batter to the pan and the remainder to the bowl. Level the surfaces and bake them in a preheated oven at 325°F (160°C, Gas 3). Allow 50 minutes for the bowl and about 1 hour for the pan. Transfer to a wire rack to cool.

Cover the board: Roll out the green fondant on a surface dusted with confectioners' sugar and use it to cover the cake board (see page 17).

Toadstool base: Cut a little cake away from the bottom of the round cake to shape the toadstool base. Halve the cake and sandwich the layers together with a little buttercream. Measure the circumference of the cake with a piece of string. Frost the sides of the cake with more buttercream and position slightly to one side of the board. Roll out the white fondant and trim to a strip that is the length of the string and ½ inch (1 cm) wider than the depth of the cake. Secure the strip around the cake, pressing the ends together where they meet at the back and smoothing the edge of the fondant over the top of the cake. Frost the top with more buttercream.

Toadstool top: Frost the top of the pudding bowl cake with the remaining buttercream. Roll out the red fondant to a 10-inch (25 cm) circle and use it to cover the cake. Tuck the edges of the fondant underneath the cake and set it on the toadstool base. Thinly roll out the white fondant trimmings and cut out a few disks using the cutters. Secure in place on the top with a dampened paintbrush.

Door and windows: Roll out the brown fondant and cut out a 2½ x 1½-inch (6 x 3.5 cm) rectangle. Make grooves with the back of a knife and position for a door. Roll and position two 1¼-inch (3-cm) squares of yellow fondant for windows. Roll out the pink fondant. Cut out and position thin strips to make door and window frames. Secure a yellow candy to the door using the decorator frosting, to form a doorknob.

Garden: Shape and secure flattened disks of yellow fondant for a garden path. Pipe lines of green decorator frosting for trailing flower stems. Finish by securing sugarcraft flowers around the toadstool.

Pirate Ship

Ingredients

- 6-inch (15-cm) round quantity rich chocolate cake batter (see page 9)
- Vanilla buttercream (see page 11), plus an extra half quantity
- 1½ oz (40 g) unsweetened cocoa powder
- 10-inch (25-cm) round cake board
- 3 lattice-shaped chocolate bars
- Selection of small round gummy candies
- Blue food coloring
- Small piece gray rolled fondant
- 2 chocolate mint sticks
- 8 caramel candies
- Tubes of black and white decorator frosting
- Round, chocolate-coated honeycomb toffee candies

Equipment

- 8½ x 4½ x 2½-inch (1.3 litre) loaf pan, lined with parchment paper (see page 23)
- Sharp knife
- Metal spatula
- Sheet of black paper
- Hole puncher
- Fine paintbrush

Bake the cake: Spoon the cake batter into the pan and level the surface. Bake in a preheated oven at 325°F (160°C, Gas 3) for 1 hour, or until cooked through. Let cool on a wire rack.

Ship: Divide the larger quantity of buttercream between 2 bowls and beat the unsweetened cocoa powder and 1 tablespoon boiling water into one bowl. Cut the domed crust off the top of the cake. Curve off the corners vertically at the front of the cake into a point. Cut out a small slab from the center of the cake. Discard a third of this and position the larger piece at the back of the cake, securing in place with a little chocolate buttercream. Place on the board and frost as smoothly as possible with the remaining chocolate buttercream. Mark planks of "wood" onto the sides of the ship with a knife. Use the lattice-shaped chocolate bars to make rails, cutting to fit and pressing down gently into the buttercream to hold them in place. Secure the small gummy candies for portholes.

Sea: Beat a little blue food coloring into the half quantity of vanilla buttercream and spread all over the cake board, using the edge of a metal spatula to create a "rough sea." Shape small triangular shapes in gray fondant and position on the sea for shark fins.

Sails: Cut out 3 rectangles measuring 3¾ x 3 inches (9 x 7 cm) in black paper. Punch holes at the sides of the paper and make one long side of each ragged by cutting into it with scissors. Thread 2 rectangles onto one of the chocolate mint sticks. Soften the caramels if very hard (see page 21). Mold 2 together and push a hole down through the center with the end of the paintbrush. Push the mint stick down into the caramel to hold it upright and secure it to the cake. Assemble the other sail using one rectangle of paper and secure to the cake. Cut triangular pieces of black paper from the trimmings and secure around the tops of the sails with black decorator frosting.

AHOY

AHOY

AHOY

Finishing touches: Mold a cylindrical cannon shape from the remaining caramels and position on the deck with a gummy candy on either side and several round chocolate-covered honeycomb toffee candies for cannonballs. Pipe borders around the portholes and "nails" in the wood with black decorator frosting. Add foam around the front of the ship with white decorator frosting.

Watch out for the sharks!

Ballerina Shoes

Ingredients

- 1 lb (500 g) red rolled fondant
- Tube of red decorator frosting
- 8-inch (20-cm) round vanilla layer cake (see page 7)
- ⅓ cup (5 tablespoons) raspberry or strawberry jam
- Vanilla buttercream (see page 11)
- 10-inch (25-cm) round cake board
- 1¾ lb (875 g) white rolled fondant
- Confectioners' sugar, for dusting
- 2 oz (50 g) pink rolled fondant
- Edible shimmer spray (optional)
- ½-inch (5-mm) wide red ribbon, 24 inches long

Equipment

- Cookie sheet
- Parchment paper
- Metal spatula
- Rolling pin
- Fine paintbrush

Shoes: Line a cookie sheet with parchment paper. Knead 6 oz (175 g) of the red fondant into a smooth oval shape about 5 inches (12 cm) long. Push a deep cavity into the fondant to create a ballet shoe shape and place on the parchment paper. Repeat with another 6 oz (175 g) fondant. Pipe red dots around the top edges of the shoes using decorator frosting.

Cover the cake: Halve the cake horizontally and sandwich the layers together with the jam and half the buttercream, then place on the board. Frost the cake with the remaining buttercream. Reserve 2 oz (50 g) of the white fondant, then roll out the remainder on a surface dusted with confectioners' sugar and use to cover the cake (see page 16).

Cover the cake board: Roll out a further 3½ oz (100 g) of the red fondant and use to cover the surface of the board around the cake (see page 17).

Border: Roll out the remaining white and red fondant along with the pink fondant into logs about ¾ inch (1.5 cm) wide. Cut into ½-inch (1-cm) pieces and roll each into a ball. Secure around the base of the cake with a dampened paintbrush.

Finishing touches: Spray the shoes with edible shimmer spray, if using, and let dry for a few minutes. Carefully transfer the shoes to the top of the cake and secure them in place using decorator frosting. Cut the ribbon into 2 equal pieces. Tuck the ribbons around the shoes, securing in place with decorator frosting.

Try me too! See page 48

Real ribbon ties!

Pretty matching border!

Super Spaceship

Ingredients

- 8-inch (20-cm) round quantity rich chocolate cake batter (see page 9)
- Vanilla buttercream (see page 11)
- 12-inch (30-cm) round cake board
- 1½ lb (750 g) dark blue rolled fondant
- Confectioners' sugar, for dusting
- 1 oz (25 g) each white, orange, and yellow rolled fondant
- Small piece strawberry-flavored lace
- Red and edible silver food colorings
- Tube of white decorator frosting
- Silver or blue dusting powder
- Birthday candles (optional)

Equipment

- 2-quart (2-litre) ovenproof pudding bowl, lined with baking parchment (see page 24)
- Sharp knife
- Metal spatula
- Rolling pin
- Paintbrush
- Pencil and paper
- Parchment paper
- Small star cutter

Bake the cake: Add the cake batter to the lined bowl and level the surface. Bake in a preheated oven at 325°F (160°C, Gas 3) for 1¼ hours, or until cooked through. Let cool on a wire rack.

Cover the cake: Slice off any domed crust from the cake so it sits flat when inverted. Slice horizontally into thirds and sandwich the layers together with half the buttercream. Place on the cake board and frost the cake with the remaining buttercream. Roll out the blue fondant to a 14-inch (35 cm) circle on a surface dusted with confectioners' sugar. Dampen the surface of the cake board around the cake using a paintbrush. Lift the fondant over the cake and ease it around the sides and down onto the board. Dust your hands with confectioners' sugar and use your palms to smooth the fondant out flat. Trim off the excess around the outside edge of the board.

Rocket: Trace and cut out the rocket template on page 127. Roll out the white fondant and cut around the template. Transfer to a piece of parchment paper and leave to harden for several hours.

Planets: Take ½ oz (15 g) each of the orange and yellow fondant and roll into 2 thin sausages. Roll and bend the two together several times so the colors marble together. Shape into a ball and flatten until about 2 inches (5 cm) in diameter. Secure to the cake with a dampened paintbrush. Roll a ½-oz (15 g) ball of blue fondant trimmings and flatten in the same way. Secure to the cake and indent with the end of the paintbrush to create craters. Shape a small orange-and-yellow marbled planet in the same way. Cut a piece of strawberry lace and secure it across the middle of the planet before securing the planet to the cake.

Stars: Thinly roll out more blue fondant trimmings and cut out stars using the small star cutter. Secure in place on the cake, adding some to the board as well.

Finishing touches: Decorate the rocket with strips of strawberry lace, paint it with red and edible silver food coloring, and then secure it to the cake using decorator frosting. Pipe clusters of distant stars with decorator frosting. Paint the cratered planet and stars with edible silver food coloring. Dip a dry paintbrush in the dusting powder and flick gently over various areas of the cake to add sparkle. Arrange birthday candles, if using, around the cake board, or push them into the cake behind the rocket.

Glittery rocket boosting candles!

Knitty Kitty

Ingredients

- 7-inch (18-cm) round quantity vanilla Madeira cake batter (see page 10)
- 5 oz (150 g) bright blue rolled fondant
- Confectioners' sugar, for dusting
- 9-inch (23-cm) round cake board
- Vanilla buttercream (see page 11)
- Red food coloring
- 5 oz (150 g) strawberry-flavored laces
- 8 oz (250 g) black rolled fondant
- 2 oz (50 g) white rolled fondant
- Black food coloring

Equipment

- 2 x 2½-cup (700-ml) ovenproof pudding bowls, lined with parchment paper (see page 24)
- Pastry brush
- Rolling pin
- Sharp knife
- Metal spatula
- Fine paintbrush

Bake the cake: Divide the cake batter evenly between the bowls, level the tops, and bake them in a preheated oven at 325°F (160°C, Gas 3) for 50 minutes, or until cooked through. Let cool on a wire rack.

Cover the board: Roll out the blue rolled fondant on a surface dusted with confectioners' sugar and use to cover the board (see page 17).

Ball of wool: Remove the cakes from their bowls and cut a slice off the top of each so when the cakes are put together they form a neat sphere. Sandwich the cakes together with a third of the buttercream. Color the remaining buttercream red and frost the spherical cake in an even layer. Take long pieces of strawberry lace and wrap them around the cake, pressing them gently into the buttercream. Once you've used about half the laces, halve the remaining laces and use them to fill in the gaps, pushing the ends into the buttercream to hold them in place. Carefully lift the cake and set onto the center of the board.

Kitten: Use the black rolled fondant. First roll a 4-oz (125-g) piece into an egg shape. Flatten the pointed end down and position on top of the wool. Cut a ¾-oz (20-g) piece of fondant in half and roll each into a log, flattening at one end. Tuck the flattened ends under the body for front legs, securing with a dampened paintbrush. Roll 2 slightly larger log shapes and position for back legs. Roll a 2½-oz (65-g) ball of fondant for the head and press into place, then thinly roll a ½-oz (15-g) piece of fondant for a tail. Taper it until thin at one end and add a contrasting tip using white fondant. Add two pointed black ears with smaller triangles of white fondant in the center of each. Roll 4 small cherry-sized balls of fondant, indent them with paw shapes using the back of a knife, and secure one at the end of each leg.

Try me too! See page 92

Meeeeeeeeeooooow!

Face: Flatten a pea-sized ball of white fondant into a very thin oval shape and press vertically onto the face. Add a smaller oval of fondant across this, pinching out the center, and secure. Paint facial details with black and red food coloring using a fine paintbrush. Drape a piece of strawberry lace over the kitten to finish.

Miss Millipede

Ingredients

- Green, red, yellow, and blue food colorings
- Double quantity vanilla buttercream (see page 11)
- 16 x 12-inch (40 x 30 cm) rectangular cake board
- ¾ cup (150 g) granulated sugar
- 12 chocolate or vanilla cupcakes baked in white paper baking cups or red, blue, and yellow ones (see page 8)
- 24 fruit chews
- 24 strawberry pencils, each 2½ inches (6 cm) long
- 2 hard mint candies
- Tube of red decorator frosting
- Small piece of white rolled fondant
- Blue food coloring
- 1½ oz (40 g) blue rolled fondant
- Confectioners' sugar, for dusting
- Small handful of mini candy-coated chocolates

Equipment

- Metal spatula
- Fine paintbrush
- Rolling pin
- 1¾-inch (4-cm) round cutter

Base: Beat a little green food coloring into a quarter of the buttercream and spread all over the board.

Millipede: Divide the sugar among three small bowls. Add a dash of red food coloring to one bowl. Press the back of a teaspoon against the coloring to work the color into the sugar. Once the color is distributed, blend it evenly by rubbing the sugar between your fingers. Color the sugars in the other bowls yellow and blue. Frost the cupcakes with the remaining buttercream, doming it up in the center and spreading it as smoothly as possible with a metal spatula. Roll a third of the cupcakes in the red sugar, a third in the yellow, and a third in the blue. Arrange in a curved line on the base.

Legs: Use your fingers to mold the fruit chews into oval shapes and place one either side of each cupcake. If the chews are very brittle, soften in the microwave first (see page 21). Push one end of each strawberry pencil into the side of a cupcake and the other end onto the chew to shape legs and feet.

Facial features: For eyes, secure the mint candies to the front cupcake using decorator frosting. Secure a small semicircular piece of white fondant for the mouth, and then outline the mouth with the decorator frosting. Paint the eyes blue using a paintbrush and a little blue food coloring, diluted slightly with water.

Hat: Roll out a little of the blue fondant on a surface dusted with confectioners' sugar and cut out a circle using the cutter. Secure to the top of the face cupcake. Shape the remaining blue fondant into a top hat and secure in place.

Finishing touches: Pipe small flowers onto the base with decorator frosting, pushing a mini candy-covered chocolate into the center. Add a flower to the millipede's hat.

Stretchy chewy legs!

Cute candy face!

Turn over to meet Miss Millipede's best friend...

Ladybug

Ingredients

- Double quantity 6-inch (15-cm) round vanilla layer cake batter (see page 7)
- ⅓ cup (5 tablespoons) raspberry or strawberry jam
- Vanilla buttercream (see page 11)
- 8-inch (20-cm) round cake board
- 1 lb (500 g) pale green rolled fondant
- Confectioners' sugar, for dusting
- 2 oz (50 g) deep green rolled fondant
- 3½ oz (100 g) red rolled fondant
- 2 oz (50 g) black rolled fondant
- Small piece white rolled fondant
- ¾-inch (2-cm) wide red ribbon with white polka dots, 24 inches (60 cm) long

Equipment:

- 3 x 6-inch (15-cm) round cake pans, lined with parchment paper (see page 22)
- 3-cup (750 ml) ovenproof pudding bowl, lined with parchment paper (see page 24)
- Sharp knife
- Metal spatula
- Rolling pin
- ½-, ¾-, and 1¼-inch (1-, 2-, and 3-cm) round cutters

Bake the cakes: Divide the batter evenly among the pans and the bowl and bake them in a preheated oven at 350°F (180°C, Gas 4). Allow 25 minutes for the cake pans and 35 minutes for the bowl. Transfer to a wire rack to cool.

Shape the cakes: Slice off the domed surface of the pudding bowl cake so it sits flat when inverted. Trim a little off of the sides to make an oval shape. Layer the 3 cakes together with the jam and a third of the buttercream. Invert onto the cake board. Frost the top and sides with more buttercream, reserving some for the ladybug.

Cover the cake: Roll out the pale green fondant on a surface dusted with confectioners' sugar and use to cover the cake (see page 16). Roll out the deep green fondant and use to cover the surface of the board around the cake (see page 17).

Ladybug: Frost the oval cake with the remaining buttercream. Roll out the red fondant and cut off one straight edge. Smooth onto the cake so about a quarter is left uncovered. Roll out half the black fondant, cut a straight edge, and use to cover the rest of the cake. Tuck the excess fondant under the ladybug, dampen the bottom with a paintbrush, and set on top of the cake. Roll out a little white fondant and use the ¾-inch (2-cm) cutter to cut out two circles for eyes. Roll out the remaining black fondant and use the ½-inch (1-cm) disks cutter to cut out smaller circles for the pupils, as well as different-sized disks for the spots on its back. Cut a thin strip of black fondant for the strip along the back. Lightly moisten the bottom of all the fondant decorations and secure in place on the ladybug.

Finishing touches: Secure the ribbon around the base of the cake (see page 21).

Who else is buzzing around the garden...?

Buzzing Beehive

Ingredients

- 2½ lb (1.25 kg) white rolled fondant
- Confectioners' sugar, for dusting
- Two 6-inch (15-cm) square lemon Madeira cakes (see page 10)
- Lemon buttercream (see page 11)
- 6 oz (200 g) green rolled fondant
- 11-inch (28-cm) round cake board
- Brown food coloring
- Small piece each of dark brown and yellow rolled fondant
- Large handful of white mini marshmallows
- Tube of white decorator frosting
- Several fresh flowers, to decorate

Equipment

- Rolling pin
- Sharp knife
- Cookie sheet
- Parchment paper
- Small metal spatula
- Pastry brush
- Ruler
- ¾-inch (2-cm) round cutter
- Fine paintbrush

Roof: Roll out half the white fondant. Cut out two rectangles 6¼ x 3¼ inch (16 x 7.5 cm) in size. Mark grooves along each with the back of a knife. Let harden for 24–48 hours on parchment paper.

Shape the cakes: Cut off any excess dome from the tops of the cakes so they can be pushed together without leaving too much of a gap. Cut a shallow, sloping edge from one side of each cake to shape the roof and reserve the pieces. Sandwich the cakes together with a third of the buttercream. Position so the roof is uppermost then evenly frost the cakes with the remaining buttercream, smoothing it flat with a metal spatula and positioning the cut-off pieces of sponge cake to raise the pitch of the roof.

Cover the board: Use the green fondant to cover the board (see page 17). Carefully transfer the cake to the board.

Beehive: Roll out the remaining white fondant and cut into strips 2½ inches (6 cm) wide. Measure the width of one long side of the cake and cut a panel the length of the cake along one long edge and tapering out so it's slightly wider at the other (the base). Press into position against the cake. Repeat around all sides. Cover the cake with a second layer of panels, dampening the top edges of the first layer of panels to hold the second layer in place. Repeat with a third layer of panels, remembering to add a shallow "pitch" at the tops of the end panels. Use the round cutter to press a circle into the fondant at the front of the hive near the roof. Paint the circle dark brown using brown food coloring.

Bees: Roll a small, cherry-sized ball each of dark brown and yellow fondant. Stretch into oval shapes and cut each into six. Reassemble into ovals, alternating the yellow and brown colors. Make two small cuts at the top of each with the tip of the knife. Slice the marshmallows, squeeze them flat between your fingers, and push them into the cuts. Paint tiny faces using brown food coloring. Repeat until you have about 14 bees.

Finishing touches: Carefully peel away the paper from the roof sections. Dampen the edges around the top of the beehive and rest the roof pieces on top. Pipe white decorator frosting along the pitch of the roof to hold the roof sections together. Secure the bees all over the hive using the decorator frosting and add a few fresh flowers to the board to decorate.

Squidgy marshmallow wings!

Bee-autiful fresh flowers!

Beedazzling!

Elephants on Parade

Ingredients

- 8-inch (20-cm) round quantity rich chocolate cake batter (see page 9)
- 6 oz (175 g) milk chocolate, broken into pieces
- Pastel-colored sugar sprinkles
- 2 oz (50 g) white chocolate, broken into pieces
- 2 oz (50 g) pale pink rolled fondant
- Confectioners' sugar, for dusting
- White chocolate ganache (see page 13)
- 5 oz (150 g) pale green rolled fondant
- 9-inch (23-cm) round cake board

Equipment

- Empty 1lb 12oz (800 g) food can, lined with parchment paper (see page 24)
- 7-inch (18-cm) round cake pan, lined with parchment paper (see page 22)
- Pencil and paper
- Parchment paper
- Cookie sheet
- 3 paper pastry bags (see page 20)
- Rolling pin
- Metal spatula
- 2-inch (5-cm) round cutter

Bake the cakes: Pour 10 oz (300 g) of the cake batter into the food can and add the remainder to the cake pan. Level the surfaces and bake in a preheated oven at 325°F. (160°C, Gas 3) Allow 35 minutes for the small cake and about 50 minutes for the large cake. Transfer to a wire rack to cool.

Shape the elephants: Trace the elephant templates on page 127 onto separate pieces of paper. Slide each piece under separate sheets of parchment paper, each set on a cookie sheet. Melt the milk chocolate (see page 14). Spoon a third into a paper pastry bag and snip off the very end point (see page 21). Pipe over the outlines of the elephants until you've piped 6 elephants facing left and 9 facing right (see page 19). Put more chocolate in another pastry bag and snip off a slightly larger end point. Flood the centers of the elephant outlines with the chocolate. Once you've filled 3 shapes, sprinkle them generously with sugar sprinkles. (The excess can be tipped away once the shapes have set.) Repeat on the remainder.

Decorate the elephants: Trace and cut out the ear template. Melt the white chocolate, add to the third pastry bag, and snip off the end point. Thinly roll a little of the pink fondant on a surface dusted with confectioners' sugar, place the ear template on the fondant, and cut out around it. Secure in place with some white chocolate from the bag.

Cover the cakes: Place the large cake on the board and frost it with a generous half of the white chocolate ganache. Position the small cake on top and frost with the remainder.

Cover the cake board: Roll out a third of the pale green fondant and use to cover the surface of the board around the cake (see page 17).

Canopy: Thinly roll out half the remaining pale green fondant and cut out a circle using the can as a guide. Use a knife to mark the circle into 8 evenly spaced wedges. Use the cutter to cut out a scalloped edge from the circle by cutting semicircles from between the wedges. Set the canopy on top of the cake. Use the remaining pale green fondant to cover the top outer edge of the large cake.

Fondant canopy!

Finishing touches:
Carefully peel the paper away from the elephants and secure them around the side of the cakes. Pipe lines of white chocolate over the knife marks on the canopy. Roll pea-sized balls of pink fondant and secure at the tips of the canopy with a dampened paintbrush. Position a larger ball of pink fondant in the center.

Candy-speckled elephants!

Street Sneakers

Ingredients

- 7-inch (18-cm) square vanilla Madeira cake (see page 10)
- 5 oz (150 g) pale brown rolled fondant
- Confectioners' sugar, for dusting
- 9-inch (23-cm) square cake board
- Half quantity vanilla buttercream (see page 11)
- 15 oz (475 g) purple rolled fondant
- 5 oz (150 g) white rolled fondant
- 1½ oz (40 g) black rolled fondant
- 2 black licorice laces

Equipment

- Sharp knife
- Pastry brush
- Rolling pin
- Metal spatula
- Pencil and paper
- Fine paintbrush
- ½-inch (1-cm) round cutter

Shape the cake: Cut a ¾-inch (2-cm) vertical slice off one side of the cake. Cut the large piece of cake in half. Round off the square corners of the two rectangles. Cut a slanting slice off each rectangle that starts a third of the way along each rectangle and slopes down to the toe end of the sneakers. Slice off the top edges of the cake where you've cut the slopes to complete the sneaker shapes.

Cover the board: Roll out the brown fondant on a surface dusted with confectioners' sugar and use to cover the board (see page 17).

Sneakers: Frost the cakes with the buttercream. Roll out 13 oz (400 g) of the purple fondant and cut out two rectangles, each 12½ inches (32 cm) long and ¼ inch (5 mm) wider than the depth of the back of the sneakers. Wrap the rectangles around the cakes so the cut ends rest about 1 inch (2.5 cm) back from the toes. Roll out two-thirds of the white fondant to a 5-inch (12 cm) round and cut in half. Secure to the fronts of the sneakers so the cut sides meet the purple fondant. Fit the white fondant around the front and trim off the excess. Carefully transfer the cakes to the board. Roll the black fondant into 2 circles and press into the heel ends. Trace and cut out the sneaker templates on page 127. Thinly roll out the remaining purple fondant and cut around the templates. Secure the tongue pieces first, then dampen the edges with a paintbrush and secure the eyelet sections. Thinly roll a small piece of white fondant and cut out circles using a ½-inch (1-cm) cutter. Mark 10 evenly spaced circles on each sneaker and push a hole in the center of each with the end of the paintbrush. Thinly roll out long strips of white fondant and secure around the bases of the sneakers, adding a slightly thicker strip of white around the fronts.

Try me too! See page 86

Sweet sneakers!

Laces: Cut the strips of licorice long enough to lace up the eyelets of the sneakers but insert 4 longer pieces of licorice into the top eyelets and leave them dangling.

Licorice laces!

Calling all cool dudes... 👉

Flamin' Skateboard

Ingredients

- 10 oz (300 g) gray rolled fondant
- Confectioners' sugar, for dusting
- 9 oz (275 g) black rolled fondant
- 14 x 10-inch (35 x 25 cm) cake board
- Two 6-inch (15 cm) square vanilla Madeira cakes (see page 10)
- Vanilla buttercream (see page 11)
- 1 lb (500 g) orange rolled fondant
- 5 oz (150 g) red rolled fondant
- 2 chocolate mint sticks, each 4 inches long
- 3½ oz (100 g) purple rolled fondant
- Tube of black decorator frosting
- 4 brown candy-coated chocolates
- Edible silver food coloring

Equipment

- Rolling pin
- Pastry brush
- Sharp knife
- Metal spatula
- Pencil and paper
- Fine paintbrush

Cover the board: Roll 7½ oz (225 g) of the gray fondant on a surface dusted with confectioners' sugar into a thick sausage with your hands and do the same with 2 oz of the black fondant. Lay the black fondant over the gray and roll the two out together. Fold over and reroll, and repeat plenty of times until the gray fondant is streaked with black. Use to cover the cake board (see page 17). Let harden for several hours.

Shape the cake: Slice the tops off the cakes so they are 1½ inches (3.5 cm) deep. Halve the cakes horizontally and sandwich the layers together with half the buttercream. Round off 4 corners to create a skateboard shape. Invert the cakes onto the cake board making sure the straight edges are together and the tops are completely level, then frost with the remaining buttercream.

Skateboard: Roll out the remaining black fondant, cut out strips and cover the sides of the cake. This is easiest to do in sections. Make a template by drawing a rectangle measuring 12 x 6 inches (30 x 15 cm) onto paper. Round off the corners as you did with the cake. Roll out the orange fondant until large enough to set the template on top. Cut out and place over the top of the cake.

Flame: Trace and cut out the flame template on page 126. Set this onto the skateboard template so the flame area fills about two-thirds of the template. Cut this template out. Thinly roll out the red fondant and cut around the flame template. Transfer to the cake, lifting the edges and securing in place with a dampened paintbrush.

Wheels: Thinly roll out a little gray fondant and cut out two 2-inch (5 cm) squares. Secure them at either end of the skateboard. Press the end of a pencil into the corners. Divide 1 oz (30 g) of gray fondant in half, shape 2 gray blocks, and place them over the squares. Thinly roll the remaining gray fondant and use it to cover the chocolate mint sticks. Position these on the blocks. Shape 4 wheels from purple fondant and press them onto the ends of the sticks.

Finishing touches: Use decorator frosting to pipe around the edges of the flames and to pipe a brick pattern onto the board. Attach the brown candies to the wheels using decorator frosting and paint the gray wheel supports with edible silver food coloring.

wheeeeeeeeeeeee!

Candy Bag

Ingredients

- 6-inch (15 cm) round rich chocolate cake (see page 9)
- 3½ oz (100 g) deep red rolled fondant
- Confectioners' sugar, for dusting
- 8-inch (20 cm) round cake board
- Dark chocolate ganache (see page 13)
- 11 oz (325 g) brown rolled fondant
- 2 oz (50 g) white rolled fondant
- Variety of candies, for decoration

Equipment

- Sharp knife
- Pastry brush
- Rolling pin
- Metal spatula
- Fine paintbrush

Shape the cake: Cut a thin vertical slice from one side of the cake so it can be set on its side without falling over. Cut another thin slice from the opposite side of the cake and stand the cake on its side. Slice off the edges of the cake (where the base was) so the back and front of the cake have slightly curved edges.

Cover the board: Roll out the red fondant on a surface dusted with confectioners' sugar and use to cover the board (see page 17).

Bag: Spread a little chocolate ganache onto the center of the board and set the cake on it. Frost the cake with the remaining ganache. Knead 1 oz (25 g) of the brown fondant with the white fondant until evenly colored. Cut the remaining brown fondant in half and roll out each piece to a rectangle that measures roughly 7 x 5 inches (18 x 12 cm). Thinly roll out the pale brown fondant. Cut very thin strips from the pale brown fondant and arrange over the darker brown fondant, spacing the strips ½ inch (1 cm) apart. Carefully roll with a rolling pin so the strips become flattened (see page 18). Roll the rectangles until you're able to trim them down to rectangles measuring roughly 9½ x 6 inches (24 x 15 cm). Drape one rectangle around the back of the cake and one around the front, dampening the inside of the fondant edges where they meet with a paintbrush and pinching them together to create a bag shape.

Finishing touches: Pile the candies into the top of the bag, scattering some around the bottom on the cake board.

Try me too! See page 56

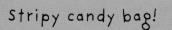

Stripy candy bag!

Life is sweet!

Now let's go to the movies...

Popcorn Box

Ingredients

- 8-inch (20 cm) square vanilla Madeira cake (see page 10)
- ⅓ cup (75 g) dulce de leche or other caramel sauce
- Vanilla buttercream (see page 11)
- 4 oz (125 g) deep blue rolled fondant
- Confectioners' sugar, for dusting
- 8-inch (20 cm) round cake board
- 2 lb (1 kg) white rolled fondant
- 5 oz (150 g) pink rolled fondant
- 7 oz (200 g) caramel popcorn

Equipment

- Sharp knife
- Metal spatula
- Pastry brush
- Rolling pin
- Paper pastry bag
- Fine paintbrush
- 1¾-inch (4-cm) and 2-inch (5-cm) round cutters
- 1-inch (2.5-cm) star cutter

Shape the cake: Slice off the domed crust of the cake so it's level with the top edges of the cake. Cut the cake vertically into quarters. (Wrap one quarter and freeze to use another day.) Beat the caramel sauce into the buttercream and use some to sandwich the layers of the cakes together.

Cover the board: Roll out the blue fondant on a surface dusted with confectioners' sugar and use to cover the board (see page 17). Carefully transfer the cake to the board.

Box: Half fill a pastry bag with more buttercream and set aside (see page 21). Use the remainder to frost the sides of the cake with a metal spatula. Roll out the white fondant and cut a strip that's the same as the depth of the cake. Cut panels of fondant to fit the sides of the cake. Lift into position. (Dampen the edges of the first panel with a paintbrush to help the other sides stay in place). Thinly roll the pink fondant and cut ¼-inch (5-mm) wide strips. Secure these around the sides of the box.

Label: Using the white fondant trimmings, roll out, then stamp out a circle using the 2-inch (5-cm) cutter, and stamp out a star using the star cutter. Reroll the pink fondant trimmings and stamp out a circle using the 1¾-inch (4-cm) cutter. Reroll both circles to stretch them into oval shapes. Now cut a star out of the center of the pink oval. Slot the white star into the pink oval star-shaped hole. Secure the pink oval to the white oval to make the label, and secure to the cake.

Popcorn: Cut off the end point of the pastry bag so the buttercream flows out in a thick line. Pipe plenty on top of the cake and press the caramel popcorn gently into position to make a pile. Secure some popcorn onto the board with more buttercream.

POP! POP!

POP!

Real popcorn pieces!

Jelly Bean Surprise

Ingredients

- 3½ oz (100 g) each red, pink, and green rolled fondant
- Confectioners' sugar, for dusting
- 7-inch (18-cm) round quantity vanilla Madeira cake batter (see page 10)
- White chocolate ganache (see page 13)
- 8-inch (20-cm) round cake board
- 3 oz (75 g) yellow rolled fondant
- 10 oz (300 g) jelly beans

Equipment

- Parchment paper
- Rolling pin
- Sharp knife
- 6-inch (15-cm) round cake pan, lined with parchment paper (see page 22)
- Metal spatula
- Fine paintbrush

Fondant covering: Line a cookie sheet with parchment paper. Roll out the red, pink, and green fondants on a surface dusted with confectioners' sugar and cut out 9 rectangles measuring 3¾ x ½ inches (9 x 1 cm). Transfer to the paper. Reroll the trimmings to make extras. You'll need about 48 in total. Let harden for several hours or overnight.

Bake the cake: Add the cake batter to the pan and level the surface. Bake in a preheated oven at 325°F (160°C, Gas 3) for 1–1¼ hours, or until cooked through. Let cool on a wire rack.

Shape the cake: Slice the cake horizontally into three and sandwich the layers together with half the chocolate ganache. Place the cake on the board and frost with the remaining ganache.

Cover the cake board: Roll out the yellow fondant and use to cover the surface of the board around the cake (see page 17). Arrange the strips of colored fondant vertically around the sides of the cakes, alternating the colors, pressing them gently into the ganache.

Finishing touches: Pile the jelly beans on top of the cake to cover the ganache completely.

Fancy fondant strips!

All your favorite jelly beans!

There's another surprise in store...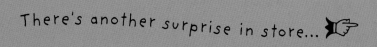

Perfect Present

Ingredients

- Two 6-inch (15-cm) square lemon Madeira cakes (see page 10)
- Lemon buttercream (see page 11)
- 5 oz (150 g) lemon curd
- 10-inch (25-cm) round cake board
- 2 lb (1 kg) lime green rolled fondant
- Confectioners' sugar, for dusting
- 4 oz (125 g) navy blue rolled fondant
- 7 oz (200 g) white rolled fondant

Equipment

- Sharp knife
- Metal spatula
- Rolling pin
- Fine paintbrush

Cover the cake: Cut off any excess dome from the tops of the cakes so they can be sandwiched together without leaving too much of a gap. Split each cake in half horizontally and sandwich all the layers back together with half the buttercream and the lemon curd to shape a cube. Place the cake on the board and frost with the remaining buttercream, filling the gaps between the cakes to shape an evenly frosted cube. Roll out the lime green fondant on a surface dusted with confectioners' sugar to a 12-inch (30-cm) circle and use to cover the cake (see page 16). Smooth the fondant down around the sides and pinch the excess together at the corners. Trim this fondant off with a knife as well as the excess fondant around the base. Smooth down as neatly as possible.

Cover the board: Use navy blue fondant to cover the surface of the board around the cake (see page 17).

Ribbon: Thinly roll out the white fondant. Cut out 4 strips that are 1¾ inch (4 cm) wide and long enough to extend over the sides of the cakes. Position them so they meet in the center at the top. Cut out 2 strips measuring 3 x 1¾ inches (7 x 4 cm) and set these on top of the cake for the bow ends. Roll and cut out 2 further rectangles measuring 5 x 1¾ inches (12 x 4 cm). Bend them into a loop and set on top of the cake, pinching the cut ends together to complete the bow. Cut a small square of fondant and place in the center of the bow for the knot. You might need to push pieces of crumpled paper towels into the loops to hold the shape until the fondant hardens.

Simply beautiful!

Macaron Gift Box

Ingredients

- 7-inch (18-cm) square rich chocolate cake (see page 9)
- 9-inch (23-cm) square cake board
- White chocolate ganache (see page 13)
- Four 3½ oz (100 g) or 4 oz (125 g) white chocolate bars, each measuring 7½ x 3¾ inches (19 x 9 cm)
- 3½ oz (100 g) pale green rolled fondant
- Confectioners' sugar, for dusting
- 20 French macarons
- 20 mini paper baking cups
- 1¾-inch (4-cm) wide pastel-colored ribbon, 60 inches (1.5 m) long

Equipment

- Sharp knife
- Metal spatula
- Fine paintbrush
- Rolling pin

Box: Slice off the top of the cake if domed in the center and invert onto the cake board. Frost the cake with the chocolate ganache. Press a bar of white chocolate against each side of the cake to make a box shape.

Cover the cake board: Roll out the green fondant on a surface dusted with confectioners' sugar and use to cover the edges of the board (see page 17).

Assembling: Place the macarons in paper baking cups and arrange in rows in the box. Wrap the ribbon around the sides of the box and tie in a bow at the front.

Try me too! See page 74

It's a box made of chocolate!

Neat rows of macarons!

Bunting Bonanza

Ingredients

- 7-inch (18-cm) round quantity vanilla Madeira cake batter (see page 10)
- Vanilla buttercream (see page 11)
- ⅓ cup (5 tablespoons) raspberry or strawberry jam
- 1¾ lb (875 g) pale blue rolled fondant
- Confectioners' sugar, for dusting
- 9-inch (23-cm) round cake board
- 5 oz (150 g) ivory rolled fondant
- ½-inch (1-cm) wide pink ribbon, 40 inches (1 m) long
- Tube of white decorator frosting
- White piping cord, 47 inches (1.5 m) long
- 3 oz (75 g) pink rolled fondant

Equipment

- 6-inch (15-cm) round cake pan, lined with parchment paper (see page 22)
- 1lb 12oz (800 g) empty food can, lined with parchment paper (see page 24)
- Sharp knife
- Metal spatula
- Rolling pin
- Fine paintbrush

Bake the cakes: Spoon 8 oz (250 g) of the cake batter into the food can and the remainder into the pan. Level the surfaces and bake them in a preheated oven at 325°F (160°C, Gas 3). Allow 35 minutes for the cake in the can and 50–55 minutes for the cake in the pan. Let cool on a wire rack.

Cover the cakes: Cut off the domed crust from the tops of the cakes. Split the cakes horizontally and sandwich the layers with a third of the buttercream and the jam. Invert the cakes and frost them with the remainder. Cover the large cake with 1 lb (500 g) of the pale blue fondant (see page 16). Cover the smaller cake with the remaining fondant, reserving the trimmings. Position the large cake on the board and sit the smaller cake on top of the larger cake.

Cover the cake board: Use 3 oz (75 g) of the ivory fondant to cover the surface of the board around the cake (see page 17). Tie lengths of the pink ribbon around the sides of the cakes and use a dot of decorator frosting from the tube to secure them in place.

Cord: Pipe a dot of decorator frosting at the end of the piping cord and push it gently into the center of the top cake. Trail the cord over the side of the cake and loop it in a gentle curve until it meets the top of the lower cake. Cut the piping cord and secure it in place at frequent intervals using decorator frosting. Position 3 further pieces of piping around the sides of the large cake, securing them in the same way.

Bunting: Thinly roll out the ivory fondant trimmings. Take a pea-sized piece of pink fondant and roll it under your finger until no thicker than a piece of fine string. Using the tip of a small knife cut off the smallest amount you can and dot it onto the ivory fondant. Repeat until the fondant is closely speckled with pink dots. Gently roll the pink fondant into the ivory (see page 18). Cut the fondant into ¾-inch strips (2-cm), then cut across the strips, angling each cut to make bunting triangles. Secure the bunting triangles to the cake using a dampened paintbrush, leaving a space slightly longer than one of the triangles. Thinly roll out the remaining pink fondant and speckle it with ivory fondant in the same way. Roll a pea-sized ball of blue fondant under your finger until no thicker than a piece of fine string. Loop around the ivory fondant to create an irregular pattern. Roll the colors into the pink fondant, cut into triangles, and secure as before.

Fancy fondant bunting!

Queen of Cakes

Ingredients

- 7 oz (200 g) deep yellow rolled fondant
- Confectioners' sugar, for dusting
- Edible gold food coloring
- 8-inch (20-cm) round quantity vanilla Madeira cake batter (see page 10)
- ⅓ cup (5 tablespoons) raspberry or strawberry jam
- Vanilla buttercream (see page 11)
- 9-inch (23-cm) round cake board
- 1½ lb (750 g) white fondant
- 7 oz (200 g) deep red fondant
- Tubes of red and white decorator frosting
- Miniature sugar pearls

Equipment

- Parchment paper
- Pencil and paper
- Rolling pin
- ¾-inch (2-cm) flower plunger cutter
- Fine paintbrush
- 1½-cup (350-ml) capacity ovenproof pudding bowl, lined with parchment paper (see page 24)
- 7-inch (18-cm) round cake pan, lined with parchment paper (see page 22)
- Metal spatula

Crown frame: Line a small cookie sheet with parchment paper. Trace four of the crown templates (see page 127) onto more parchment paper. Roll out 3½ oz (100 g) of the yellow fondant on a surface dusted with confectioners' sugar, and cut out four strips measuring 5½ x ¾ inch (14 x 1.5 cm). Arrange each strip, on its side, over the marked template so they set in a curved shape.

Flowers: Thinly roll out a further 3 oz (75 g) of the remaining yellow fondant and cut out flowers using the cutter. You'll need about 30 altogether. Place them on the parchment paper around the crown frame and let harden for 48 hours. Paint the crown frame and flowers with edible gold food coloring and let dry for another couple of hours.

Bake the cake: Pour 7½ oz (225 g) of the cake batter into the pudding bowl and add the remainder to the cake pan. Bake them in a preheated oven at 325°F (160°C, Gas 3), allowing 45 minutes for the pudding bowl and 1 hour 10 minutes for the pan. Let cool on a wire rack.

Cover the cake: Split the larger cake horizontally and sandwich the layers together with the jam and half the buttercream. Invert onto the cake board and frost with all but ¼ cup (4 tablespoons) of the remaining buttercream. Roll out the white fondant and use to cover the cake (see page 16).

Cover the cake board: Roll out 3 oz (75 g) of the red fondant and use to cover the surface of the board around the cake (see page 17).

Crown: Frost the small cake with the reserved buttercream. Roll out the remaining red fondant to an 8½-inch (21-cm) circle and use to cover the cake, tucking the ends underneath. Dampen the edges that are tucked underneath and set onto the larger cake.

Assemble the cake: Place a cherry-sized ball of yellow fondant on top of the crown. Carefully place the four pieces of the crown's frame around the crown, securing at the base and on top with a dot of red decorator frosting. Thinly roll out the remaining yellow fondant to a ¾-inch (2-cm) strip and secure around the base of the red fondant. Set another ball of yellow fondant on top of the crown, pinching it to a point at the top. Paint the top decoration and the crown base with edible gold food coloring. Using white decorator frosting, secure the flowers evenly around the base of the cake and secure the sugar pearls around the sides. Then secure a sugar pearl in the center of each flower.

Royally good!

Golden flowers fit for a queen!

Japanese Blossom

Ingredients

- 2 teaspoons rosewater
- Vanilla buttercream (see page 11)
- 8-inch (20-cm) round vanilla layer cake (see page 7)
- ¼ cup (4 tablespoons) raspberry or strawberry jam
- 10-inch (25-cm) round black cake board
- 1½ lb (750 g) pale gray rolled fondant
- Confectioners' sugar, for dusting
- 3½ oz (100 g) white rolled fondant
- Brown food coloring
- 3 oz (75 g) deep pink rolled fondant
- Tube of white decorator frosting

Equipment

- Sharp knife
- Metal spatula
- Rolling pin
- Fine paintbrush

Cover the cake: Beat the rosewater into the buttercream. Halve the cake horizontally and sandwich the layers together with the jam and half the buttercream, then invert onto the cake board. Frost the cake with the remaining buttercream. Roll out the gray fondant on a surface dusted with confectioners' sugar and use to cover the cake (see page 16).

Cover the cake board: Use the white fondant to cover the surface of the board around the cake (see page 17).

Tree: Dilute a little of the brown food coloring in a small bowl with ⅛–¼ teaspoon water. Use a paintbrush to paint a twisted tree shape, with the trunk emerging from the bottom of one side of the cake, bending and curving into finer branches across the top.

Blossom: Pinch off tiny pieces of pink fondant and shape into teardrop-shaped petals. Arrange in circles on the tree branches to form blossoms, securing with a dampened paintbrush. Set some petals singularly or in clusters of 2 or 3. Pipe dots of white decorator frosting into the center of each blossom and scatter a few dots around the blossoms. Scatter blossoms onto the cake board and down the sides of the cake, if you wish.

Golden Sunflowers

Ingredients

- 7-inch (18-cm) square rich chocolate cake (see page 9)
- 10-inch (25-cm) square cake board
- Chocolate buttercream (see page 11)
- 5 oz (150 g) green rolled fondant
- Confectioners' sugar, for dusting
- 4-oz (125-g) package milk chocolate finger cookies
- 16 small round chocolate-coated cookies
- Double quantity royal icing (see page 12)
- Yellow and orange food colorings

Equipment

- Metal spatula
- Rolling pin
- Sharp knife
- Fine paintbrush
- Several paper pastry bags (see page 20)
- Leaf tip

Cover the cake: Place the cake on the board. Reserve a quarter of the buttercream and frost the cake with the remainder.

Field: Thinly roll out 4 oz of the green fondant on a surface dusted with confectioners' sugar. Cut into strips 1 inch wide. Dampen the surface of the board surrounding the cake with a paintbrush and lay a strip along each side of the cake so the strips overlap at the corners. Miter the fondant at the corners, remove the excess, and smooth the fondant down. Use more buttercream to cover the gap between the cake and the fondant. Use the edge of the metal spatula to mark deep vertical lines around the sides of the cake.

Sunflowers: Press 4 chocolate finger cookies vertically into each side of the cake. Halve the remaining finger cookies and scatter over the top of the cake. (These will help support the round cookies and can be moved around when you arrange them). Spread a little buttercream under each round cookie and arrange over the cake, propping them up at different angles. Color the royal icing sunflower yellow using the yellow and orange food colorings. Half fill a paper pastry bag fitted with a leaf tip (see page 21). Pipe an irregular band of icing around the sides of a cookie, then build up extra layers of petals by making smaller blobs of icing and pulling the tip away to make them slightly ragged. Repeat on all the remaining cookies, fitting the tip into a clean pastry bag once each bag has been emptied.

Leaves: Thinly roll out the remaining green fondant and cut out slender leaf shapes. Secure to the bottom of the chocolate finger "stalks" with a dampened paintbrush.

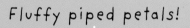

Fluffy piped petals!

Crisp cookie centers!

Chocolate finger stalks!

What else is growing... ☞

Window Box Blooms

Ingredients

- 7-inch (18-cm) round quantity Madeira cake batter (see page 10)
- 3½ oz (100 g) white chocolate, broken into pieces
- 16 chocolate mint sticks
- 6–8 large pink and white marshmallows
- Pastel-colored candy-coated chocolates
- Large handful of mini pink and white marshmallows
- Sugar sprinkles
- Pastel-colored mini candy-coated chocolates
- 5 oz (150 g) lilac rolled fondant
- Confectioners' sugar, for dusting
- 9-inch (23-cm) round cake board
- Chocolate buttercream (see page 11)
- 1 lb (500 g) brown rolled fondant
- 2 oz (50 g) semisweet chocolate

Equipment

- 8½ x 4½ x 2½-inch (1.3 litre) loaf pan, lined with parchment paper (see page 23)
- Two large cookie sheets
- Parchment paper
- Pastry brush
- Rolling pin
- Sharp knife
- Fine paintbrush

Bake the cake: Add the cake batter to the pan and bake in a preheated oven at 325°F (160°C, Gas 3) for 1¼ hours, or until cooked through. Let cool on a wire rack.

Marshmallow flowers: Line a large cookie sheet with parchment paper. Melt the white chocolate (see page 14). Place a chocolate mint stick on the paper and spoon a blob of white chocolate over the end so it spreads to about 1¼ inches (3-cm) wide and resembles a small lollipop. Snip a large marshmallow across into thin pieces to create petal shapes. Press onto the melted chocolate to create a flower, adding a candy-coated chocolate to the center. Make 4 more in the same way. Cut 3 chocolate mint sticks down to 3 inches (7.5 cm) and make 3 more flowers in the same way, spreading the melted chocolate to a ¾-inch (2-cm) circle and using the mini marshmallows for petals. Use sugar sprinkles for the centers. Make another 5–6 flowers using the mini marshmallows but without the chocolate stalks.

Chocolate flowers: Line another cookie sheet with parchment paper. Make 5 tall-stemmed flowers and 3 short-stemmed flowers in the same way as above but using candy-coated chocolates and mini candy-coated chocolates instead of the marshmallows. Fill the centers with sugar sprinkles. Make extra flowers without stalks.

Cover the board: Use the lilac fondant to cover the cake board (see page 17).

Box: Trim off the edges of the cake so the sides are vertical. Halve horizontally and sandwich the layers together with a third of the chocolate buttercream. Carefully transfer the cake to the board. Frost the cake with the remaining buttercream. Roll out the brown fondant and cut out rectangles the same size as the sides of the cake. Secure in place, dampening the edges of the fondant with a paintbrush where the sections meet to hold them together. Make vertical marks all over the fondant with the back of a knife.

Finishing touches: Melt the semisweet chocolate. Carefully peel the paper away from the flowers and press the chocolate sticks down into the cake, positioning the larger flowers at the back and the shorter ones at the front. Press the flowers without stalks around the front and sides of the box. Dot a little melted chocolate onto the backs of a few and secure to the front of the box and the board.

Vegetable Garden

Ingredients

- 8-inch (20-cm) square rich chocolate cake (see page 9)
- 10-inch (25-cm) square cake board
- 3½ oz (100 g) pale brown rolled fondant
- Confectioners' sugar, for dusting
- Dark chocolate ganache (see page 13)
- 4-oz (125-g) package white chocolate finger cookies
- 3½ oz (100 g) semisweet chocolate, finely grated
- 3½ oz (100 g) green rolled fondant
- 4 round green candies, about ½ inch (1 cm) in diameter
- 4 orange fruit chews
- 3 vanilla fruit chews
- Green food coloring
- 4 chunks soft fudge
- 8 pink candy-covered chocolates
- Tube of white decorator frosting

Equipment

- Fine paintbrush
- Rolling pin
- Sharp knife
- Metal spatula

Cover the board: Place the cake on the board. Thinly roll out the pale brown fondant on a surface dusted with confectioners' sugar and use to cover the area of the board surrounding the cake (see page 17).

Cover the cake: Frost the cake evenly with the chocolate ganache, but let it spill slightly onto the brown fondant border.

Fence: Press the white chocolate finger cookies upright around the walls of the cake.

Soil: Sprinkle the grated chocolate all over the top of the cake, allowing some to fall down between the fencing.

Cabbages: Flatten a pea-sized piece of green fondant between your finger and thumb to make a leaf shape. Press against the side of a round green candy. Shape another leaf shape and press against the candy, overlapping slightly with the first. Continue to layer 8–9 more leaf shapes to build up a cabbage. Repeat on the remaining 3 candies.

Carrots: Soften an orange fruit chew (see page 21). Cut into 3 pieces and shape each into a carrot. Mark grooves around the carrots with a knife. Shape tiny leaves in green fondant and secure to the tops with a dampened paintbrush. Make about 8 carrots altogether.

Leeks: Soften a vanilla fruit chew as before. Flatten as thinly as possible and cut in half. Make cuts along one long edge with the tip of a knife, then roll up each piece. Dilute a little green food coloring with water and brush over the ends of the leeks, smudging the color with your fingertip.

Potatoes: Soften a piece of fudge in the same way as the chews. Mold into small irregular pieces to shape potatoes.

CRUNCH

CRUNCH

CRUNCH

Radishes: Shape small leaves in green fondant and secure to the tops of the pink candies with a dampened paintbrush.

Finishing touches: Arrange the vegetables in rows over the soil. Finish the fence by piping the decorator frosting in curved lines to link the finger cookies.

CRUNCH

Watch out for rabbits!

Funky Flowers

Ingredients

- Two 6-inch (15-cm) square lemon Madeira cakes (see page 10)
- Lemon buttercream (see page 11)
- 8-inch (20-cm) square cake board
- 2 lb (1 kg) white rolled fondant
- Confectioners' sugar, for dusting
- 8 oz (250 g) lime green rolled fondant
- 7 oz (200 g) pale orange rolled fondant
- Selection of brightly colored fresh flowers, such as daisies
- Tube of white decorator frosting

Equipment

- Sharp knife
- Metal spatula
- Rolling pin
- Fine paintbrush

Shape the cake: Cut off any excess dome from the tops of the cakes so they can be sandwiched together without leaving too much of a gap. Split each cake in half horizontally and sandwich the layers together with half the buttercream to shape a cube. Place the cake on the board and frost it with the remaining buttercream, filling in the gaps between the cake layers to shape an evenly frosted cube.

Cover the cake: Roll out the white fondant on a surface dusted with confectioners' sugar to a 12-inch (30-cm) circle and use to cover the cake (see page 16). Smooth the fondant down around the sides and pinch the excess together at the corners. Trim off this fondant, and the fondant around the base, using a knife. Smooth down as neatly as possible.

Cover the board: Use 3 oz (75 g) of the lime green fondant to cover the surface of the board around the cake (see page 17).

Stripes: Thinly roll out the remaining green and the orange fondant and cut out ½-inch (1 cm) wide strips long enough to extend from the base of the cake and up over the top edge. Secure in place with a dampened paintbrush.

Flowers: Cut the flower stalks down to 2 inches in length and wrap the ends in plastic wrap. Arrange them on top of the cake, securing them in place with decorator frosting.

Fabulous fresh flowers!

Funky fondant colors!

Yoga Student

Ingredients

- Confectioners' sugar, for dusting
- 2 oz (50 g) each black and flesh-colored rolled fondant
- 3½ oz (100 g) green rolled fondant
- 9-inch (23-cm) round lemon Madeira cake (see page 10)
- ½ cup (6 tablespoons) lemon curd
- Lemon buttercream (see page 11)
- 11-inch (28-cm) round cake board
- 1¾ lb (875 g) white rolled fondant
- 5 oz (150 g) purple rolled fondant
- 6 oz (175 g) blue rolled fondant
- 1 oz (25 g) milk chocolate, broken into pieces
- Brown food coloring
- 3 oz (75 g) orange rolled fondant
- Tube of white decorator frosting

Equipment

- Cookie sheet
- Parchment paper
- Sharp knife
- Toothpick
- Rolling pin
- Fine paintbrush
- Fine cheese grater
- Paper pastry bag (see page 20)
- Flower plunger cutters in various sizes

Yoga student: Line a cookie sheet with parchment paper. On a surface dusted with confectioners' sugar, roll the black fondant into a ball, then flatten it out roughly to a rectangle, about 3½ inches (8 cm) long and tapering almost to a point at one end. Make a slit from the thin end to the center to create legs. Bend the thick end into a sitting position and cross the legs at the front. Place on the parchment. Flatten a cherry-sized ball of flesh-colored fondant and place on top. Push a small hole into the front with a toothpick. Shape 1 oz (25 g) of the green fondant into a t-shirt shape, accentuating the arms, and secure in place. Roll a cherry-sized ball of flesh-colored fondant and position for the head. Take a similarly sized piece of fondant, cut in half, and shape each into an arm. Secure in place, sliding pieces of crumpled paper towels under the hands to hold the arms in place until hardened. Let harden overnight.

Cover the cake: Cut the domed crust off of the top of the cake. Halve the cake horizontally and sandwich the layers together with the lemon curd and half the buttercream. Invert the cake onto the board and frost with the remaining buttercream. Roll out the white fondant and use to cover the cake (see page 16).

Cover the cake board: Roll out 3½ oz (100 g) of the purple fondant and use to cover the surface of the board around the cake (see page 17).

Mat: Thinly roll out 3½ oz (100 g) of the blue fondant until large enough to cut out a neat rectangle measuring 6½ x 3½ inches (17 x 8 cm). Press a fine cheese grater all over the surface to create texture. Cut out the rectangle and set it onto the cake. Transfer the yoga student to the mat, securing in place with a dampened paintbrush.

Hair and face: Melt the chocolate (see page 14). Add it to a paper pastry bag, cut off the end point (see page 21) and use it to pipe hair. Paint closed eyelids and a mouth using brown food coloring.

Flowers: Use the remaining blue, green, and purple fondant, and the orange fondant to cut out flowers in various sizes using the flower plunger cutters (see page 19). Secure in place around the sides of the cake using decorator frosting. Add a few more to the top of the cake and pipe more decorator frosting into the center of each flower.

Wow! Lotus position!

Tasty textured mat!

Cupcake Tower

Ingredients

- 1 lb (500 g) deep red rolled fondant
- Confectioners' sugar, for dusting
- 12-inch (30-cm) round cake board
- Triple quantity vanilla cupcakes, baked in red and pink paper baking cups (see page 8)
- Double quantity vanilla buttercream (see page 11)
- 8 oz (250 g) each pink and burgundy rolled fondant
- 1½ lb (750 g) soft fruits e.g. small strawberries, raspberries, and blueberries

Equipment

- Pastry brush
- Rolling pin
- Sharp knife
- Metal spatula
- 3-inch (7-cm) round cutter

Cover the board: Roll out 8 oz (250 g) of the red fondant on a surface dusted with confectioners' sugar and use to cover the cake board (see page 17).

Cupcakes: Frost the cupcakes with the buttercream, doming up the mixture slightly in the center.

Frosting: Thinly roll out the remaining red fondant and cut out circles using the cutter. Place a circle over a third of the cupcakes, fitting the fondant neatly around the edges. Roll out the pink and burgundy fondants and use to cover the remaining cupcakes. Use different colored baking cups that contrast with the fondant tops, so you end up with varying color combinations. Let firm up overnight.

Assembly: Arrange 12 cupcakes on the cake board, placing them compactly together. Arrange a circle of 8 cupcakes for the second tier, then 5 for the third tier, 3 for the fourth tier, and placing a single cupcake on the top. (There will be 7 cupcakes remaining that you won't need in the stack). Shortly before serving (and once the cake is placed in its serving position), scatter the fruits around the tiers of the cupcakes and on the cake board.

Try me too! See page 40

MMMMMMMMMMMMMMMMM!!

Cocktail Time

Ingredients

- 8-inch (20-cm) round vanilla layer cake (see page 7)
- ⅓ cup (5 tablespoons) lemon curd
- Lemon buttercream (see page 11)
- 11-inch (28-cm) round cake board
- 1¾ lb (750 g) white rolled fondant
- Confectioners' sugar, for dusting
- 3½ oz (100 g) deep blue rolled fondant
- 1 oz (25 g) red rolled fondant
- 3½ oz (100 g) orange rolled fondant
- Tubes of red and white decorator frosting
- 2 candy sticks
- 3½ oz (100 g) lime green rolled fondant
- 3½ oz (100 g) yellow rolled fondant
- 5 candied cherries

Equipment

- Sharp knife
- Metal spatula
- Rolling pin
- Fine paintbrush
- Pencil and paper
- Toothpick
- 2-inch (5-cm) and 1¾-inch (4-cm) round cutters

Cover the cake: Slice the cake in half horizontally and sandwich the layers together with the lemon curd and half the buttercream. Place on the board and frost with the remaining buttercream. Roll out the white fondant on a surface dusted with confectioners' sugar and use to cover the cake (see page 16).

Cover the cake board: Roll out the blue fondant and use to cover the surface of the board around the cake (see page 17).

Cocktail: Trace and cut out the cocktail glass and umbrella templates on pages 126–7. Place the glass template on the cake so the base is near one edge and make an outline of the glass on the white fondant with the tip of a toothpick. Remove the template and cut out the 2 dotted-line sections. Roll out a little red fondant and cut out the lower section of the glass. Secure in place with a dampened paintbrush. Roll out a little of the orange fondant, cut out the other section of the template, and secure it in place. Pipe red decorator frosting over the outline of the glass.

Umbrella and straw: Thinly roll out the blue fondant trimmings and cut out the umbrella shape. Halve one candy stick and position it at the top of the glass, adding the umbrella at the end. Position the other candy cane for the straw.

Fruits: Roll out the green and yellow, and remaining orange fondants and cut out circles with the cutters. Cut some of the circles in half. Arrange them all around the sides of the cake, adding one circle at the top of the glass, and secure in place. Halve the candied cherries and use a dot of decorator frosting to secure them in place around the fruits, adding a couple to the top of the glass.

Finishing touches: Pipe white decorator frosting over all of the fruits to resemble cut sides and to decorate the umbrella. Pipe a wavy line of red frosting down the straw.

Frosted, not stirred!

Cheers!

Fruity fondant!

Vintage Birdcage

Ingredients

- 8-inch (20-cm) round quantity lemon Madeira cake batter (see page 10)
- ¼ cup (4 tablespoons) lemon curd
- Lemon buttercream (see page 11)
- 2 round cake boards, 8-inch (20-cm) and 10-inch (25-cm) diameters
- 13 oz (400 g) soft green rolled fondant
- Confectioners' sugar, for dusting
- Tube of white decorator frosting
- 6 oz (175 g) pale pink rolled fondant
- 3½ oz (100 g) each white and deep pink rolled fondant
- Small ornamental bird, to decorate

Equipment

- 6-inch (15-cm) round cake pan, lined with parchment paper (see page 22)
- 1-quart (1-litre) ovenproof pudding bowl, lined with parchment paper (see page 24)
- String
- Sharp knife
- Metal spatula
- Fine paintbrush
- Rolling pin

Bake the cakes: Divide the cake batter equally between the pan and the bowl. Level the surfaces and then bake them in a preheated oven at 325°F (160°C, Gas 3) for 1 hour, or until both are cooked through. Let cool on a wire rack.

Shape the cakes: Measure the circumference of the cake with string. Slice off the domed crust from the cakes so there's not too much of a gap between the cakes when stacked together. Sandwich the two cakes together with the lemon curd and half the buttercream. Vertically trim off the sides of the bowl cake to make a birdcage shape with straight sides. Place the cake on the smaller board and frost as smoothly as possible with the remaining buttercream, using the metal spatula.

Cover the cake boards: Roll out 3 oz (75 g) of the green fondant on a surface dusted with confectioners' sugar and use to cover the surface of the board around the cake (see page 17). Now dot the larger board with a little decorator frosting and position the cake and smaller board on top. Cover the bare surface of the larger board with some of the pale pink fondant.

Cage: Knead the remaining green fondant with the white fondant to lighten the color. Thinly roll out a little and cut out two strips the same length as the string and ¾ inch (1.5 cm) wide. Secure one strip around the base of the cake and the other around the top. Thinly roll out more of the fondant and cut out ½-inch (1-cm) wide lengths. Position a vertical strip against the cake, securing it to the fondant at the base and top of the cake with a dampened paintbrush and trimming off any excess at the top of the dome. Repeat all around the sides, spacing the strips about 1 inch (2.5 cm) apart. Tidy up the strips where they meet at the top. Shape two small balls of fondant from the trimmings and secure them to the top of the dome.

Finishing touches: Take a pea-sized ball of pale pink fondant and roll it under your fingers until 2½ inches (6 cm) in length. Flatten lightly and then roll up to make a simple rose shape. Make about 60 more roses using the pale and deep pink fondant, with some of the roses slightly smaller and some slightly larger. Pipe trailing lines of white frosting down the sides of the cake and secure the flowers in place using a little frosting. Decorate the cage with further piping and finish by securing the ornamental bird.

Death by Chocolate

Ingredients

- 6 oz (175 g) purple rolled fondant
- Confectioners' sugar, for dusting
- 9-inch (23-cm) round cake board
- Two 6-inch (15-cm) round rich chocolate cakes (see page 9)
- Chocolate buttercream (see page 11)
- 1½ lb (750 g) brown rolled fondant
- Several chunky pieces of milk or semisweet chocolate
- 3½ oz (100 g) semisweet chocolate, broken into pieces

Equipment

- Pastry brush
- Rolling pin
- Sharp knife
- Metal spatula
- String
- Fine paintbrush

Cover the cake board: Roll out the purple fondant on a surface dusted with confectioners' sugar and use to cover the board (see page 17). Let harden for several hours.

Cover the cakes: Cut off any domed crust from the cakes. Halve each cake horizontally and sandwich all the layers together with half the buttercream. Measure the circumference of the cake with string. Position the cake slightly off-center on the board and frost with the remaining buttercream. Roll out a third of the brown fondant to a circle the same diameter as the cake. Lift on top of the cake and smooth down gently. Roll out the remaining fondant so it's large enough to cut out a rectangle the same length as the string and equal to the depth of the cake. Wrap this around the cake, securing the ends together with a dampened paintbrush and smoothing down gently with the palms of your hands.

Chocolate: Arrange a cluster of chocolate chunks near the top edge of the cake (on the side where there's a larger area of cake board). Shortly before serving, melt the broken chocolate (see page 14), then leave to cool for 5 minutes. Spoon the chocolate over the chocolate chunks so it cascades down the side to make a puddle of melted chocolate on the board. Spoon smaller quantities of chocolate onto the top edge of the cake in one or two other places so they drizzle down the other sides.

Try me too! See page 114

Flip-flops

Ingredients

- 8-inch (20-cm) square vanilla Madeira cake (see page 10)
- ½ cup (6 tablespoons) strawberry jam
- Vanilla buttercream (see page 11)
- 10-inch (25-cm) square cake board
- 2 lb (1 kg) pale pink rolled fondant
- Confectioners' sugar, for dusting
- 1 lb (500 g) gray rolled fondant
- 7 oz (200 g) deep pink rolled fondant
- 4 strawberry-flavored pencils
- Tubes of gray and edible silver decorator frosting

Equipment

- Sharp knife
- Metal spatula
- Rolling pin
- Fine paintbrush
- Pencil and paper
- ¾-inch (2-cm) heart-shaped cutter
- Ruler
- Toothpick
- ¾–1-inch (2–2.5-cm) flower plunger cutter

Cover the cake: Slice off the domed crust of the cake. Split in half horizontally and sandwich the layers together with the jam and a generous half of the buttercream. Invert onto the cake board and frost the cake with the remaining buttercream. Then roll out the pale pink fondant on a surface dusted with confectioners' sugar and use to cover the cake (see page 16).

Cover the board: Use 4 oz (125 g) of the gray fondant to cover the surface of the board around the cake (see page 17).

Flip-flops: Trace and cut out the flip-flop template on page 126. Cut a second template from the first so you have a pair. Roll out the remaining gray fondant until only just large enough to fit the two templates. Thinly roll out a little deep pink fondant and cut out hearts with the cutter. Arrange over the gray fondant and roll very lightly so the hearts are flattened into the gray (see page 18). Lay the templates over the fondant and cut around them. Transfer to the cake, dampening the fondant underneath very lightly to secure them. Trim the strawberry pencils to 4 inches (10 cm) in length. Push two ends down near the front of the flip-flops and bend the other ends over to the sides. Secure in place with gray decorator frosting and let set.

Flowers: Using a ruler and tip of a toothpick, mark a line of horizontal dots around the sides of the cake. Use the gray decorator frosting to pipe vertical lines, spaced at 1-inch (2.5-cm) intervals starting from the base of the cake up to each dot in the line. Thinly roll out the remaining deep pink fondant and cut out flowers using the plunger cutter (see page 19). Secure the top of each gray line with a little decorator frosting, saving 2 for the front of each flip-flop.

Finishing touches: Position the flip-flops on the cake and secure in place with a little decorator frosting. Use the edible silver decorator frosting to pipe the centers of the flowers and decorative piping over the flip-flops.

Here comes the sun!

Strawberry flavor straps!

What is a girl's favorite accessory...?

Chic Purse

Ingredients

- 5 oz (150 g) deep pink rolled fondant
- Confectioners' sugar, for dusting
- 9-inch (23-cm) round cake board
- 7-inch (18-cm) square vanilla Madeira cake (see page 10)
- ⅓ cup (5 tablespoons) raspberry or strawberry jam
- Vanilla buttercream (see page 11)
- 1½ lb (750 g) white rolled fondant
- 3½ oz (100 g) each deep red and orange rolled fondant
- 3 oz (75 g) black rolled fondant
- Edible gold balls
- Edible silver food coloring
- 4 x 9-inch (23-cm) pieces of licorice lace

Equipment

- Pastry brush
- Rolling pin
- Sharp knife
- Metal spatula
- 2-inch (5-cm) and 1¼-inch (3-cm) flower-shaped cookie cutters
- Fine paintbrush

Cover the cake board: Roll out the pink fondant on a surface dusted with confectioners' sugar and use to cover the board (see page 17).

Shape the cake: Cut off a quarter of the cake and discard (or eat later). Cut off the domed crust so the top is completely flat. Turn the cake on its side and cut away 2 sloping edges from the long sides, then the ends to create a purse shape. Lay the cake flat, halve it horizontally, and sandwich the layers together with the jam and a third of the buttercream. Set the cake upright, transfer it to the board, and frost with the remaining buttercream.

Purse: Roll out a third of the white fondant until it measures about 6¾ inches (17 cm) square. Thinly roll out a third of the red and orange fondant and cut out flower shapes using the cutters. Position the shapes on the white fondant, leaving irregular spaces in between. Roll out tiny balls of the black fondant and press into the centers of the flowers. Gently roll the colored fondant into the white (see page 18). Measure the end sections of the purse, cut the fondant to fit, and press gently into position. Roll out another third of the white fondant to a rectangle of about 8 x 6½ inches (20 x 16 cm). Decorate with flowers as above, then trim the shape so it fits one side of the cake. Secure it in place, stretching or cutting the fondant as required so it fits neatly. Repeat on the other side with the remaining fondants. Press the edible gold sugar balls into the centers of the flowers.

Zipper: Thinly roll out a ½-inch (1-cm) wide strip of black fondant until it is 8 inches (20 cm) long. Mark a shallow groove down the center, then across the strip to represent a zipper. Secure along the top of the bag so the ends fall slightly down the sides. Paint with edible silver food coloring. Roll out another ½-inch (1-cm) wide strip to 9 inches (23 cm) and cut it in half lengthwise. Place each slightly to one side of the zipper, joining up the ends at the sides of the purse.

Handles: Thinly roll out 4 pieces of black fondant to 1-inch (2.5 cm) squares. Secure 2 to one side of the purse and push a vertical slit through the center of each and into the cake. Twist 2 pieces of licorice lace together and push the ends into the black fondant on one side of the cake so the licorice is held in place. Repeat on the other side.

Bags full of flavor!

Fashionably edible!

Bollywood Dreams

Ingredients

- 8-inch (20-cm) round quantity lemon Madeira cake batter (see page 10)
- ½ cup (6 tablespoons) lemon curd
- Lemon buttercream (see page 11)
- 9-inch (23-cm) round cake board
- 1½ lb (700 g) purple rolled fondant
- Confectioners' sugar, for dusting
- 4 oz (125 g) bright blue rolled fondant
- 11-inch (28-cm) round cake board
- Tube of white decorator frosting
- 12 oz (375 g) orange rolled fondant
- Edible gold balls
- Edible gold food coloring
- Blue mini candy-coated chocolates

Equipment

- 7-inch (18-cm) round cake pan, lined with parchment paper (see page 22)
- Empty 1 lb 12 oz (800 g) food can, lined with parchment paper (see page 24)
- Metal spatula
- Rolling pin
- Fine paintbrush
- 1-inch (2.5-cm) heart-shaped cutter

Bake the cakes: Add 8 oz (250 g) of the cake batter to the food can and add the remainder to the pan. Level the surfaces and bake in a preheated oven at 325°F (160°C, Gas 3), allowing about 35 minutes for the small cake and 50–60 minutes for the large. Let cool on a wire rack.

Fill the layers: Cut the domed crust off the top of each cake. Halve each cake horizontally and sandwich the layers back together with the lemon curd and half the buttercream. Invert the larger cake onto the smaller board and frost with two-thirds of the remaining buttercream.

Lower tier: Roll out 1¼ lb (625 g) of the purple fondant on a surface dusted with confectioners' sugar and use to cover the cake (see page 16).

Cover the cake boards: Roll out 3 oz (75 g) of the blue fondant and use to cover the surface of the smaller board around the cake (see page 17). Dot the larger board with a little decorator frosting and position the cake and smaller board on top. Cover the edges of the larger board with 3 oz (75 g) of the orange fondant.

Top tier: Frost the small cake with the remaining buttercream, cover with the remaining orange fondant, and carefully position on the larger cake. Thinly roll out the remaining blue fondant to a long thin strip measuring 12 inches long and ¾ inch (1.5 cm) wide. Secure around the base of the top tier with a dampened paintbrush.

Dome: Shape a further 3½ oz (100 g) of the purple fondant into a ball. Flatten slightly and pinch the top into a point to create a dome shape. Secure to the top of the cake.

Finishing touches: Thinly roll out the remaining purple fondant and cut into 1-inch (2.5-cm) wide strips. Cut out shapes with the lower two-thirds of the heart cutter. Secure around the base of the lower tier. Gently press vertical rows of edible gold balls into the fondant, securing in place with decorator frosting from the tube. Paint the shapes and the dome with edible gold food coloring. Press the blue candies into the top tier leaving gaps of about 1¼ inches (3 cm) between each. Press 3 gold balls around the edge of each. Press more gold balls around the base of the dome, the base of the top tier, and around the large board.

Golden glamor!

Bling!

Look who's having a snooze... 🖝

Sleepy Puppy

Ingredients

- 7-inch (18-cm) round quantity vanilla Madeira cake batter (see page 10)
- 6 oz (175 g) ivory rolled fondant
- Confectioners' sugar, for dusting
- 10-inch (25-cm) round cake board
- Half quantity vanilla buttercream (see page 11)
- 7 oz (200 g) deep red rolled fondant
- Tube of white decorator frosting
- 11 oz (325 g) pale brown rolled fondant
- Small piece of black rolled fondant
- 3 oz (75 g) blue rolled fondant
- 1 oz (25 g) yellow rolled fondant
- Brown food coloring

Equipment

- 7-inch 18-cm) round cake pan, lined with parchment paper (see page 22)
- 3-cup (700-ml) ovenproof pudding bowl, lined with parchment paper (see page 24)
- Pastry brush
- Rolling pin
- Sharp knife
- Metal spatula
- Fine paintbrush

Bake the cake: Add 1 lb (500 g) of the cake batter to the pan and add the remainder to the bowl. Level the surfaces and bake them in a preheated oven at 325°F (160°C, Gas 3) for 40 minutes, or until both are cooked through. Let cool on a wire rack.

Cover the board: Roll out the ivory fondant on a surface dusted with confectioners' sugar and use to cover the cake board (see page 17).

Bed: Frost the larger cake with two-thirds of the buttercream. Roll out the red fondant to a 9-inch (23-cm) circle and use to cover the cake, smoothing it to fit around the sides and trimming off the excess at the base. Carefully transfer the cake to the board, positioning it off-center. Pipe "stitches" around the bed using decorator frosting.

Dog: Cut a slice off the top of the small cake so it sits flat on the surface. Trim off the sides to make an oval shape and cut a slope down to the head end. Frost the cake with the remaining buttercream. Roll out 5 oz (150 g) of the brown fondant and cover the body. Tuck the ends underneath, then push deep grooves into the sides to indicate haunches. Set on the bed, allowing room on one side to place the head. Take another 1 oz (25 g) of the fondant and cut in half. Shape each into a ball, stretch, and flatten slightly. Make 4 cuts on one side for paws. Secure on the cake with a dampened paintbrush. Shape another 4 oz (125 g) into an oval for the head and place it over the paws. Flatten a small piece of black fondant for a nose and secure it to the dog's face. Use the tip of a knife to indent the mouth. Roll 2 small balls of ivory fondant trimmings for eyeballs. Shape a small ball of brown fondant, cut it in half, and secure the halves onto the eyeballs to make eyelids.

Blanket: Thinly roll out the blue fondant and then the yellow fondant. Cut fine strips of yellow fondant, as thinly as you can, and lay a few on the blue fondant, spaced a generous ½ inch (1 cm) apart.

Arrange more yellow strips in the opposite direction. Roll the yellow fondant into the blue (see page 18). Cut into irregular shapes and tuck around the dog.

Finishing touches: Take ½ oz (15 g) of brown fondant and cut it in half. Shape each into a long, floppy ear and attach to either side of the head. Using brown food coloring, paint pupils on the eyeballs, bristles on the muzzle, and paw prints on the cake board.

Chef's Special

Ingredients

- 8-inch (20-cm) round vanilla layer cake (see page 7)
- ¼ cup (4 tablespoons) strawberry or raspberry jam
- Vanilla buttercream (see page 11)
- 10-inch (25-cm) round cake board
- 1¾ lb (875 g) white rolled fondant
- Confectioners' sugar, for dusting
- 6 oz (175 g) navy blue rolled fondant
- 2 oz (50 g) pale brown rolled fondant
- 1 oz (25 g) gray rolled fondant
- Edible silver food coloring

Equipment

- Sharp knife
- Metal spatula
- Rolling pin
- Fine paintbrush
- Pencil and paper

Cover the cake: Halve the cake horizontally and sandwich the layers together with the jam and half the buttercream, then place on the board. Frost the cake with the remaining buttercream. Roll out 1½ lb (750 g) of the white fondant on a surface dusted with confectioners' sugar and use to cover the cake (see page 16).

Cover the cake board: Roll out 3 oz (75 g) of the remaining white fondant to a long, curved strip. Roll a long, thin strip of the navy blue fondant and cut out a ¼-inch (5 mm) wide strip. Place the blue strip down the center of the white and roll gently with a rolling pin so the blue strip is flattened into the white (see page 18). Use to cover the surface of the board around the cake (see page 17).

Apron: Trace and cut out the apron and pocket templates on page 127. Thinly roll out the remaining navy blue fondant. Reserve a small piece of the white fondant for the dishcloth and thinly roll out the remainder. Cut very thin strips from the white fondant and arrange on the blue fondant, spacing the strips ½ inch (1 cm) apart. Carefully roll with a rolling pin so the strips become flattened. Cut out the apron shape using the template as a guide. Brush the center of the cake with a dampened paintbrush. Drape the apron over the cake so the lower edge falls over the sides. Shape and position the pocket, pulling the top of the pocket open, and the apron ties.

Wooden utensils: Shape small utensils, such as a rolling pin, wooden spoons, and pastry brush, from the brown fondant and secure in place on the cake. For the pastry brush, mix a dot of white fondant with the brown for the brush end and indent with the tip of a knife.

Metal utensils: Shape small utensils such as a whisk handle, spatula, and lifter from gray fondant and secure in place. Use edible silver food coloring and a fine paintbrush to paint them silver.

Dishcloth: Thinly roll out the reserved white fondant and cut out a rectangle 3½ x 2½ inches (8 x 6 cm). Drape from the apron pocket.

Sushi Sensation

Ingredients

- 13 oz (400 g) white rolled fondant
- Confectioners' sugar, for dusting
- 8-inch (20-cm) square rich chocolate cake (see page 9)
- 10-inch (25-cm) square cake board
- Vanilla buttercream (see page 11)
- 1½ lb (750 g) deep red rolled fondant
- 4 oz (125 g) black rolled fondant
- 3½ oz (100 g) bottle green rolled fondant
- 3 pink jelly beans, halved
- Yellow and pink food coloring
- Pair of chopsticks
- 1 teaspoon liquid honey
- Tube of white deorator frosting

Equipment

- Parchment paper
- Rolling pin
- Sharp knife
- Metal spatula
- Fine paintbrush
- Fine cheese grater
- Wide-meshed sieve
- 1½-inch (3.5-cm) round cutter

Plate: Line a cookie sheet with parchment paper. Roll out 6 oz (175 g) of the white fondant on a surface dusted with confectioners' sugar until large enough to cut out a rectangle of 7½ x 5½ inches 19 x 13 cm). Transfer to the parchment paper. Roll up 2 pieces of paper towel and slide them under the ends to raise them up. Let harden for 24–48 hours.

Cover the cake: Cut off any excess dome from the top of the cake and invert onto the board. Fill any gaps at the bottom with vanilla buttercream and frost the cake with the remainder. Cover the cake with the red rolled fondant (see page 16). Carefully peel the paper away from the white fondant plate and set on top of the cake.

Cover the board: Use the black fondant to cover the edges of the board (see page 17).

Rolled sushi: Roll 4 oz (125 g) of the white fondant into a neat log shape 5½ inches (13 cm) long. Cut into 6 pieces. Thinly roll out the green fondant and texture the surface by pressing a fine cheese grater all over it. Cut out 6 rectangles measuring 4 x 1 inches (10 x 2.5 cm) and wrap them around the cylinders of white fondant, securing with a dampened paintbrush. Push a halved jelly bean down into each center. Reserve ½ oz (15 g) white fondant for the shrimp. Push the remainder through a wide-meshed sieve and arrange on top of the sushi as if rice.

Shrimp sushi: Shape another ½ oz (15 g) of the "rice" into an oval shape. Mold the reserved white fondant into a shrimp shape indenting the tail and flesh markings with the back of a knife, and set this onto the rice. Paint the shrimp with a dash of yellow and pink food coloring diluted with a drop of water.

Tuna sushi: Make a mound of rice as above. Knead a piece of red fondant from the trimmings into a little of the white fondant and flatten into an irregular shape for a slice of tuna. Set it on top of the rice. Roll a thin strip of green fondant around it, tucking the ends underneath.

Soy dressing: Cut out a circle of red fondant using the cutter. Wrap a strip of black fondant around it.

Assembling: Arrange the sushi, bowl, and chopsticks on the plate, securing everything with the decorator frosting. Brush the tuna and shrimps very lightly with honey to create a sheen effect.

Burger and Fries

Ingredients

- 7-inch (18-cm) round quantity vanilla Madeira cake batter (see page 10)
- 7½ oz (225 g) red rolled fondant
- Confectioners' sugar, for dusting
- 10-inch (25-cm) cake board
- 1 small store-bought Madeira cake
- Vanilla buttercream (see page 11)
- 1¼ lb (625 g) pale brown rolled fondant
- ½ teaspoon sesame seeds
- 13 oz (400 g) raisins
- 3½ oz (100 g) yellow rolled fondant
- 1 oz (25 g) lime green rolled fondant
- Red food coloring

Equipment

- 7-inch (18-cm) round cake pan, lined with parchment paper (see page 22)
- 1¾-quart (2 litre) ovenproof pudding bowl, lined with parchment paper (see page 24)
- Pastry brush
- Rolling pin
- Sharp knife
- Cookie sheet
- Parchment paper
- 2-inch (5-cm) round cutter
- Toothpick

Bake the cake: Add 14 oz (425 g) of the cake batter to the cake pan and the remainder to the bowl. Level the surfaces and bake them in a preheated oven at 325°F, (160°C, Gas 3) allowing about 40 minutes for both cakes. Let cool on a wire rack.

Cover the board: Use 6 oz (175 g) of the red fondant to cover the cake board (see page 17).

Fries: Slice any golden crust off of the store-bought Madeira cake. Cut the cake into ¾-inch (1.5-cm) slices, then into fries. Place on a cookie sheet and toast under a moderate broiler, watching closely until the cake has started to brown lightly. Turn the pieces and, when they are lightly brown, remove from the heat and let cool on a wire rack.

Burger bun: Slice any domed crust off the cakes. Frost the cake baked in the pan with a third of the buttercream. Roll out half the brown fondant to an 11-inch (28-cm) circle. Place the cake on the fondant, with the buttercream facing down, and bring the fondant up over the sides, easing to fit as neatly as possible. Place to one side of the cake board and spread with a little more buttercream. Reserve ¼ cup (4 tablespoons) of the remaining buttercream and frost the other cake with the remainder. Roll out the remaining brown fondant to a 10½-inch (27 cm) circle. Scatter with the sesame seeds and press them in firmly with the rolling pin to secure in place. Use to cover the cake, tucking the edges underneath. Transfer to a sheet of parchment paper.

Patty: Blend the raisins to a coarse paste in a food processor (or chop as finely as possible). Shape into a patty using wetted hands so the paste doesn't stick to you and position on the cake.

Cheese: Thinly roll out the yellow fondant, cut out a 6-inch (15-cm) square, and position it on the patty.

Tomatoes: Roll out the remaining red fondant ¼ inch (5 mm) thick and cut out circles using the cutter. Place on the cheese.

Lettuce: Thinly roll out the green fondant into irregular strips. Run a toothpick along one edge of each strip to frill the edge. Place on top of the tomatoes.

Ketchup: Color the reserved buttercream red and add to a paper pastry bag (see page 21). Snip off the end point and pipe wavy lines all over the lettuce. Position the burger lid on top and scatter the fries around the burger.

Beer Cooler

Ingredients

- 8-inch (20-cm) round vanilla Madeira cake (see page 10)
- Vanilla buttercream (see page 11)
- 10-inch (25-cm) round cake board
- 1½ lb (750 g) black rolled fondant
- Confectioners' sugar, for dusting
- 1 lb 2 oz (525 g) bottle green rolled fondant
- 3½ oz (100 g) yellow rolled fondant
- 3 oz (75 g) white rolled fondant
- Edible gold and silver food coloring
- Red and black food coloring
- 13 oz (40 g) clear hard candies

Equipment

- Sharp knife
- Metal spatula
- String
- Rolling pin
- Fine paintbrush
- Cookie sheet
- Parchment paper
- Pencil and paper

Ice bucket: Halve the cake horizontally and sandwich with half the buttercream. Place on the board and measure the circumference with a piece of string. Frost the cake with the remaining buttercream. Reserve 3½ oz (100 g) of the black fondant. On a surface dusted with confectioners' sugar, roll out the remainder to a strip the length of the piece of string and ½ inch (1 cm) deeper than the cake. Roll up the strip and then unroll it around the sides of the cake. Dampen the short ends with a paintbrush and lightly smooth the fondant to neaten. Let harden for 24 hours.

Bottles: Line a cookie sheet with parchment paper. Take a 3-oz (75-g) piece of the green fondant and roll it into a ball. Stretch and mold the fondant into the neck and shoulders of a beer bottle. Set it on the parchment paper and make 6 more in the same way. Let harden for 48 hours.

Cover the board: Use the yellow fondant to cover the surface of the board surrounding the cake (see page 17).

Bucket trim: Roll out the reserved black fondant to the same length as the previously rolled black fondant and ¾ inch (2 cm) thick. Brush the top edge of the black fondant with a dampened paintbrush and rest the strip over it to make a rim. Let harden for 24 hours more.

Bottle caps: Flatten small pieces of white fondant so they're ¼ inch (5 mm) wider than the tops of the bottles. Secure to the bottle tops, bending the edges over the sides. Mark indentations with the end of a fine paintbrush.

Labels: Trace and cut out the beer labels on page 126. Thinly roll out the white fondant, cut around the templates, and secure them in place on the beer bottles. Paint gold borders around the edges of the labels and simple designs in the centers using the food colorings.

Finishing touches: Paint the rim of the bucket and the bottle caps with edible silver food coloring. Carefully arrange the bottles on the cake, propping them up against some of the candies. Scatter the remaining candies around the bottles.

Pixel Cube Cake

Ingredients

- 7-inch (18-cm) square lemon Madeira cake (see page 10)
- ¼ cup (4 tablespoons) lemon curd
- Lemon buttercream (see page 11)
- 9-inch (23-cm) square cake board
- 1¾ lb (875 g) white rolled fondant
- Confectioners' sugar, for dusting
- 8 oz (250 g) black rolled fondant
- 4 oz (125 g) each pink, turquoise, yellow, gray, and lilac rolled fondant

Equipment

- Sharp knife
- Metal spatula
- Rolling pin
- Fine paintbrush

Cover the cake: Cut the domed crust off the top of the cake, then halve it horizontally and sandwich the layers together with the lemon curd and half the buttercream. Invert onto the board and frost with the remaining buttercream. Roll out 1½ lb (750 g) of the white fondant on a surface dusted with confectioners' sugar and use to cover the cake (see page 16).

Cover the cake board: Roll out 3½ oz (100 g) of the black fondant and use to cover the surface of the board around the cake (see page 17).

Pixels: Thinly roll out a third of all the colored fondants and the remaining black and white fondants and cut out ¾-inch (1.5-cm) squares. Dampen the lower half of one side of the cake with a paintbrush and position the squares along the bottom of the cake in a row. Arrange additional rows on top of the first. Continue to build up layers of squares, rolling out more fondant when you run out of squares and dampening areas of the cake as you go. Arrange the colors so some are in clusters to resemble pixels. If the rows start to become untidy or uneven, trim them in a straight line with a knife and continue to build up the squares. Continue to arrange the squares over the top and sides of the cake until you have covered 3 sides and most of the top.

Multicolored tasty pixels!

Square sensation!

Art Attack

Ingredients

- 9-inch (23-cm) round vanilla Madeira cake (see page 10)
- ⅓ cup (5 tablespoons) raspberry or strawberry jam
- Vanilla buttercream (see page 11)
- 11-inch (28-cm) round cake board
- 1¾ lb (875 g) white rolled fondant
- Confectioners' sugar, for dusting
- 4 oz (125 g) orange rolled fondant
- Squeeze of fresh lemon juice
- Royal icing (see page 12)
- Orange, yellow, black, and brown food colorings

Equipment

- Sharp knife
- Metal spatula
- Rolling pin
- Fine paintbrush

Cover the cake: Cut the domed crust off the top of the cake. Halve the cake horizontally and sandwich the layers together with the jam and half the buttercream. Invert onto the board and frost with the remaining buttercream. Roll out the white fondant on a surface dusted with confectioners' sugar and use it to cover the cake (see page 16).

Cover the cake board: Use the orange fondant to cover the surface of the board around the cake (see page 17).

Paints: Beat a little fresh lemon juice, a drop at a time, into the royal icing until it reaches the consistency of light cream. Divide among 4 small bowls or cups and color each with one of the food colorings. Test the consistency on a piece of paper. The icing should be loose enough to drizzle in thin lines with a teaspoon. If necessary, thin the icing with another drop of lemon juice.

Painting: Use a teaspoon to drizzle the brown icing back and forth over the white fondant, letting it run down the sides. The messier the lines, the more effective it will be. Repeat with the remaining colors until most of the white fondant is covered with scribbled lines.

A work of art!

Crazy paints!

Want to bet on what's over the page...?

Luck of the Draw

Ingredients

- 8-inch (20-cm) round vanilla layer cake (see page 7)
- ⅓ cup (5 tablespoons) raspberry or strawberry jam
- Vanilla buttercream (see page 11)
- 10-inch (25-cm) round cake board
- 14½ oz (450 g) deep green rolled fondant
- Confectioners' sugar, for dusting
- 1 lb 14 oz (900 g) white rolled fondant
- 5 oz (150 g) blue rolled fondant
- 7 oz (200 g) red rolled fondant
- ½-inch (1-cm) wide black ribbon, 60 inches (1.5 m) long
- Tube of white decorator frosting
- 2 oz (50 g) black rolled fondant
- Black food coloring

Equipment

- Sharp knife
- String
- Rolling pin
- Fine paintbrush
- Cookie sheet
- Parchment paper
- 1¾-inch (4-cm) and 1¼-inch (3-cm) round cutters
- Heart-, spade-, club-, and diamond-shaped cutters

Cover the cake: Measure the circumference of the cake with string. Halve the cake horizontally and sandwich the layers together with the jam and half the buttercream. Place on the board and frost with the remaining buttercream. Roll out 11½ oz (350 g) of the green fondant on a surface dusted with confectioners' sugar to a circle the same diameter as the cake. Lift it onto the cake and smooth down gently. Roll out 1 lb (500 g) of the white fondant and cut out a strip the same length as the string and the exact depth of the cake. Roll up the strip and unroll it around the side of the cake, securing the fondant together at the join with a dampened paintbrush.

Casino chips: Line a cookie sheet with parchment paper. Roll out the blue fondant, 5 oz (150 g) of the red fondant, and 5 oz (150 g) of the remaining white fondant and cut out circles using the larger cutter. Transfer to the paper and gently press the smaller cutter into the center to leave an impression. (Don't cut through completely.) Let harden for at least an hour.

Cover the cake board: Roll out the remaining green fondant and use it to cover surface of the board around the cake (see page 17).

Ribbon: Tie the ribbon around the base and the top of the cake and secure with a dot of decorator frosting.

Playing card symbols: Thinly roll out the remaining red and black fondant and stamp out playing card symbols with the cutters. Secure around the sides of the cake with a dampened paintbrush.

Pack of cards: Roll out 7½ oz (225 g) of the remaining white fondant to a thickness of ¾ inch (2 cm) and cut out a rectangle measuring 3¾ x 2½ inches (9 x 6 cm). Round off the corners to resemble a stack of cards. Push one of the playing card symbols into the center to leave an impression. Transfer to the paper.

Dice: Shape 2 small dice using the remaining white fondant.

Assemble the cake: Paint an "A" onto two corners of the card stack and paint the symbol in the center using black food coloring diluted with a little water. Secure the stack to the top of the cake. Paint small rectangles of black food coloring around the edges of all the casino chips and let dry for a few minutes. Arrange the chips in stacks of varying sizes on top of the cake, securing in place with decorator frosting. Paint the dice and secure in place.

Monsieur Mustache

Ingredients

- 7 oz (200 g) black rolled fondant
- Confectioners' sugar, for dusting
- 7-inch (18 cm) round vanilla layer cake (see page 7)
- ¼ cup (4 tablespoons) raspberry or strawberry jam
- Vanilla buttercream (see page 11)
- 9-inch (23-cm) round cake board
- 1 lb 6 oz (700 g) white rolled fondant
- Tube of black decorator frosting
- 1¼-inch (3-cm) wide black gingham or polka dot ribbon, 60 inches (1.5 m) long

Equipment

- Pencil and paper
- Cookie sheet
- Parchment paper
- Rolling pin
- Sharp knife
- Metal spatula
- Fine paintbrush

Mustache: Trace and cut out the mustache template on page 126. Line a cookie sheet with parchment paper. Thinly roll out half the black fondant on a surface lightly dusted with confectioners' sugar and cut around the template. Transfer the pieces to the parchment paper. Cut out another mustache and transfer to the paper so you have a spare in case of any breakages. Let harden overnight.

Cover the cake: Halve the cake horizontally and sandwich the layers together with the jam and half the buttercream, then place on the board. Frost the top and sides with the remaining buttercream. Roll out the white fondant and use to cover the cake (see page 16).

Cover the cake board: Roll out the remaining black fondant and use to cover the edges of the board around the cake (see page 17).

Finishing touches: Carefully peel away the paper from the mustache pieces. Pipe a little black decorator frosting onto the undersides of two pieces, position them on top of the cake, and gently press to secure. Tie the ribbon around the side of the cake and glue it in place with a dot of black decorator frosting.

Tee Time

Ingredients

- 9-inch (23-cm) round vanilla Madeira cake (see page 10)
- ⅓ cup (5 tablespoons) raspberry or strawberry jam
- Triple quantity vanilla buttercream (see page 11)
- 12-inch (30-cm) round cake board
- ¼ cup (50 g) turbinado sugar
- 1 lb (500 g) bright green rolled fondant
- Confectioners, sugar, for dusting
- Green food coloring
- 8 oz (250 g) dark green rolled fondant
- Small piece each of red and white rolled fondant
- 1 chocolate mint stick

Equipment

- Sharp knife
- Metal spatula
- Rolling pin
- 4 paper pastry bags (see page 20)
- Small star tip
- Fine paintbrush

Shape the cake: Slice the cake in half horizontally and sandwich the layers together with the jam and half the buttercream. Place on the cake board. Using a knife, cut away one edge of the cake to represent a deep bunker measuring about 5 inches (12 cm) across and as deep as the filling in the center. Cut off the edges of the cake so they're slightly rounded. Take the cut piece of cake and slice it into two irregular pieces. Secure these to the top of the cake to represent small hills. Frost the entire cake with a thin layer of buttercream.

Bunker: Sprinkle the bunker area with the turbinado sugar.

Golf course: Roll out 7 oz (200 g) of the bright green fondant on a surface dusted with confectioners' sugar and cut into an oval shape 7 inches (18 cm) long. Set on top of the cake and cut away a curve from each side so the course has a flat but irregular shape. Roll out another 3½ oz (100 g) bright green fondant to a thin, curved strip about 7 inches (18 cm) long and place on one section of the board, securing in place with a dampened paintbrush. Trim off the excess at the edge of the board.

Rough: Color the remaining buttercream green and add some to a paper pastry bag fitted with a small star tip (see page 21). Pipe small star shapes over the top of the cake not already covered with fondant or sugar, around the sides of the cake, and onto the board. Once the bag is empty, fit the second bag with the tip to complete the piping.

Bushes: Shape the remaining bright green fondant and the dark green fondant into small mounds and cone shapes. Position some on top of the cake and the rest around the sides.

Golf ball and flag: Roll the white fondant into a ball and dent all over it with the end of the paintbrush. Place in the bunker. Make a small triangular-shaped flag in red fondant and secure to the mint stick with a dampened paintbrush. Make a hole in the fondant with the end of the paintbrush and push the stick in place.

FORE! FORE! FORE! FORE!

Turn over to celebrate a new arrival...

Baby's First Cake

Ingredients

- Three 6-inch (15-cm) round vanilla layer cakes (see page 10)
- ⅓ cup (5 tablespoons) raspberry or strawberry jam
- Half quantity vanilla buttercream (see page 11)
- 9-inch (23-cm) round cake board
- 1½ lb (750 g) pale yellow rolled fondant
- Confectioners' sugar, for dusting
- 7 oz (200 g) deep yellow rolled fondant
- 4 oz (125 g) brown rolled fondant
- Brown food coloring

Equipment:

- Metal spatula
- Rolling pin
- Sharp knife
- Fine paintbrush

Cover the cakes: Sandwich the 3 cakes together with the jam and half the buttercream. Place on the cake board and frost with the remaining buttercream. Roll out the pale yellow fondant on a surface dusted with confectioners' sugar and use to cover the cake (see page 16).

Cover the cake board: Use the pale yellow fondant trimmings to cover the surface of the board around the cake (see page 17).

Stripes: Thinly roll out the deep yellow fondant and cut thin strips measuring ¾ inch (2 cm) wide and long enough to extend over the sides of the cakes and almost meet in the center at the top. Secure in place with a dampened paintbrush.

Teddy bear: Take 3 oz (75 g) of the brown fondant and shape into a smooth oval. Secure the oval in an upright position on top of the cake. Roll a smaller ball of fondant for the head and secure in place. Roll a pea-sized piece of fondant, cut it in half, and secure in place for the ears. Shape 2 chubby feet, tapering them at the ends so you can ease them under the body. Shape 2 arms, tapering them at the ends, and secure them to the teddy bear. Add a small round snout in deep yellow fondant and paint features using the paintbrush and brown food coloring diluted with a little water.

Ribbon: Thinly roll the pale yellow fondant trimmings and use to assemble a bow for the teddy bear's neck.

Try me too! See page 52

Love is in the Air

Ingredients

- Confectioners' sugar, for dusting
- 5 oz (150 g) ivory (or white chocolate-flavored) rolled fondant
- 8-inch (20-cm) round rich chocolate cake (see page 10)
- Dark chocolate ganache (see page 13)
- 10-inch (25-cm) round cake board
- 8 red roses in bloom

Equipment

- Cookie sheet
- Parchment paper
- Rolling pin
- 1 ¼–1¾-inch (3–4 cm) heart-shaped cutter
- Sharp knife
- Metal spatula
- Fine paintbrush

Hearts: Line a small cookie sheet with parchment paper. On a surface lightly dusted with confectioners' sugar, roll out 3 oz (75 g) of the ivory fondant to a ¼-inch (5-mm) thickness. Cut out 7–8 heart shapes using the cutters and transfer them to the parchment paper. Let harden for several hours or overnight.

Cover the board: Slice the cake in half horizontally and sandwich the layers together with a third of the dark chocolate ganache. Place the cake on the board and use the remaining ivory fondant to cover the surface surrounding the cake (see page 17).

Cover the cake: Frost the cake in a fairly even layer with the remaining ganache. Let stand to firm up for a couple of hours.

Finishing touches: Snip the stalks off the roses down to 2 inches (5 cm) and cover the ends in plastic wrap. Arrange on top of the cake. Peel the paper away from the fondant hearts and tuck the hearts between the flowers.

Try me too! See page 66

Love is sweet!

Romantic roses!

Get ready for a fright...

Jack-o'-Lantern

Ingredients

- 7-inch (18-cm) round quantity vanilla Madeira cake batter (see page 10)
- 5 oz (150 g) gray rolled fondant
- Confectioners' sugar, for dusting
- 9-inch (23-cm) round cake board
- Vanilla buttercream (see page 11)
- Tube of black decorator frosting
- 1¾ lb (875 g) orange rolled fondant
- Tube of yellow decorator frosting
- 1 oz (25 g) each deep green and brown rolled fondant
- 2 brown candy-coated chocolates

Equipment

- Two 4¼-cup (1 litre) capacity ovenproof pudding bowls, lined with parchment paper (see page 24)
- Pastry brush
- Rolling pin
- Sharp knife
- Metal spatula
- Pencil and paper
- Fine paintbrush

Bake the cake: Divide the cake batter equally between the pudding bowls and bake them in a preheated oven at 325°F (160°C, Gas 3) for 50 minutes, or until cooked through. Let cool on a wire rack.

Cover the board: Roll out the gray fondant on a work surface dusted with confectioners' sugar and then use to cover the board (see page 16).

Shape the cake: Cut a slice off the top of each cake so when the cakes are put together they will form a neat sphere. Halve each of the cakes horizontally and, using half the buttercream, sandwich all the layers together in a sphere shape. Frost the cake with the remaining buttercream.

Spiders web: Use the black decorator frosting to pipe the straight lines of a spider's web onto the board. Start at a point near the edge of the board so the web is off-center. Working from the center outward, pipe the curved lines of the web, distancing the curves farther apart as you work toward the outer edge of the web.

Pumpkin: Roll out the orange fondant to a circle about 12 inches (30 cm) in diameter. Drape it over the cake and fit it around the sides, easing it to fit as smoothly as possible. Pinch any areas of excess fondant together and cut them off. Smooth down the fondant with the palms of your hands and press vertical grooves at 2-inch (5-cm) intervals with your finger.

Face: Trace and cut out the pumpkin templates on page 126. Rest the mouth template on the fondant and mark around it with the tip of a sharp knife. Remove the template, cut out the mouth shape, and remove the fondant from the center. Cut out and remove the nose and eyes in the same way. Use the yellow decorator frosting to fill in the areas that have been cut out. Carefully lift the cake onto the board.

Stalk: Shape the green fondant into a pumpkin stalk, marking grooves on it with the back of a knife. Secure in place with a dampened paintbrush.

Mouse: Reserve ¼ oz (5 g) of the brown fondant and shape the remainder into a mouse. Place the mouse on the pumpkin and roll the reserved piece into a long, tapering tail. Secure the tail in position and press the brown candies onto the head for ears. Pipe eyes and whiskers onto the face using black decorator frosting.

Fall Leaves

Ingredients

- 3 oz (75 g) each deep orange, red, yellow, and leaf green rolled fondant
- Confectioners' sugar, for dusting
- 7½ oz (225 g) dark brown (or chocolate-flavored) rolled fondant
- 12-inch (30 cm) round cake board
- 8-inch (20 cm) round rich chocolate cake (see page 9)
- Dark chocolate ganache (see page 13)
- 3 oz (75 g) milk chocolate, broken into pieces

Equipment

- Two large cookie sheets
- Parchment paper
- Rolling pin
- Selection of leaf plunger cutters, in various sizes
- Pastry brush
- Sharp knife
- Metal spatula
- Paper pastry bag (see page 20)

Leaves: Line 2 large cookie sheets with tightly crumpled parchment paper. Thinly roll out the orange fondant on a surface dusted with confectioners' sugar and cut out leaf shapes using the plunger cutters (see page 19). Arrange the leaves on the crumpled paper so they harden in curved positions. Repeat with the red, yellow, and green fondants. Let harden for several hours or overnight.

Cover the board: Roll out the brown fondant and use to cover the board (see page 17).

Cover the cake: Place the cake on the board but set it slightly to one side. Frost the cake with an even layer of chocolate ganache.

Branches: Melt the chocolate (see page 14) and add to the paper pastry bag (see page 21). Snip off the end point so the chocolate flows out in a thin line. Pipe irregular branches on top of the cake and slightly down the sides.

Assembly: Gently rest a few of the smallest leaves on top of the cake. Arrange the rest of the leaves down the sides and in clusters around the base. Use a little melted chocolate from the pastry bag to hold them in place, if necessary.

wheeeeeeeeeeeee!

Skull and Bones

Ingredients

- 2 medium egg whites
- ½ cup (100 g) superfine sugar
- 7-inch (18-cm) round vanilla layer cake (see page 7)
- ¼ cup (4 tablespoons) raspberry or strawberry jam
- Vanilla buttercream (see page 11)
- 9-inch (23-cm) round cake board
- Black food coloring
- Several white mini marshmallows
- Tube of white decorator frosting

Equipment

- Cookie sheet
- Parchment paper
- Pencil and paper
- Large nylon or polythene pastry bag
- ½-inch (1-cm) plain tip
- Metal spatula

Skull and bones: Line 2 cookie sheets with parchment paper. Trace and cut out the skull template on page 127, then slide the template under the paper on one of the cookie sheets. Beat the egg whites in a large, thoroughly clean bowl until peaks form. Add the sugar, a tablespoonful at a time, whisking well between each addition until the meringue is thick and glossy. Spoon the meringue into the pastry bag fitted with the plain tip. Fill in the skull template with meringue mixture, then smooth the meringue with a metal spatula. Pipe 3-inch (7-cm) lengths of meringue onto the cookie sheets, spacing them slightly apart, and adding an extra blob at each end to create bone shapes. You'll have enough mixture to create about 20 bones. Bake the meringues in a preheated oven at 250°F (120°C, Gas ½) for about 1 hour, or until crisp. Turn off the oven. Let cool completely in the oven with the door closed.

Cover the cake: Halve the cake horizontally and sandwich the layers together with the jam and a little buttercream. Place the cake on the board, positioning it slightly to one side. Beat plenty of black food coloring into the remaining buttercream and use it to frost the cake. Cover the cake board with a thin layer of buttercream as well. Use a fork to texture the surface of the buttercream.

Finishing touches: Cut the marshmallows down into small tooth-shaped pieces and secure to the skull with the white decorator frosting. Arrange the skull and bones on top of the cake, using the decorator frosting to hold the bones in place where necessary. Pile more bones around the side of the cake.

Try me too! See page 32

Bone appetit!

Super creepy!

Wish Upon a Star

Ingredients

- 8-inch (20-cm) round vanilla layer cake (see page 7), or use a ready-made rich fruitcake, covered with marzipan instead of the jam and buttercream
- ¼ cup (4 tablespoons) raspberry or strawberry jam
- Vanilla buttercream (see page 11)
- 10-inch (25-cm) round cake board
- 2 lb (1 kg) white rolled fondant
- Confectioners' sugar, for dusting
- 3 oz (75 g) granulated sugar
- Blue food coloring
- Edible silver balls, preferably in two sizes
- 3½ oz (100 g) blue rolled fondant
- Tube of white decorator frosting
- 2-inch (5-cm) wide ribbon, about 32 inches long

Equipment

- Sharp knife
- Metal spatula
- Rolling pin
- Several star cutters, between 1¼–3¼ inches (3–7.5 cm) wide measured from point to point
- Fine paintbrush

Cover the cake: Slice the cake horizontally and sandwich the layers together with the jam and half the buttercream, then place on the board. Frost the cake with the remaining buttercream. Roll out the white fondant on a surface dusted with confectioners' sugar and use it to cover the cake (see page 16).

Stars: Use the cutters to stamp out star shapes from the top of the cake. You'll probably be able to fit 6–7 stars in total. Wipe the cutters each time you use them if they've got buttercream on them. Carefully peel away the fondant from inside the star shapes. Put the sugar in a small bowl. Add a little blue food coloring and press the back of a teaspoon against the coloring to work the color into the sugar. Once the color is distributed, rub the sugar between your fingers to ensure it is evenly blended. Spoon the sugar into the star cavities until almost full, then sprinkle in some edible silver balls.

Cover the cake board: Roll out the blue fondant and use to cover the surface of the board around the cake (see page 17).

Finishing touches: Tie the ribbon around the cake.

Snowy fondant!

Magic sprinkles!

Christmas Baubles

Ingredients

- 1¼ lb (625 g) brown rolled fondant
- Confectioners' sugar, for dusting
- 8-inch (20-cm) square rich chocolate cake (see page 9)
- Chocolate buttercream (see page 11)
- 10-inch (25-cm) square cake board
- 3½ oz (100 g) red rolled fondant
- Half quantity vanilla buttercream (see page 11)
- Red, green, and yellow food coloring
- 9 chocolate cupcakes, baked in red, green, or yellow paper baking cups (see page 8)
- 5 gummy candies, halved
- 3 strawberry-flavored laces
- Tubes of red and white decorator frosting
- Plenty of red, green, and yellow candy-coated chocolates
- Edible gold balls
- 1¾-inch (4-cm) wide ribbon, about 39 inches (1 m) long

Equipment

- Cookie sheet
- Parchment paper
- Rolling pin
- Sharp knife
- Fine paintbrush

Box: Line a cookie sheet with parchment paper. Roll out the brown fondant on a surface dusted with confectioners' sugar and cut out 4 rectangles measuring 8¼ x 3 inches (21 x 7 cm). Carefully transfer them to the paper so they retain their shape. Let harden for 24–48 hours.

Shape the cake: Cut a slice off the top of the cake so the remaining cake is 2 inches (5 cm) deep. Halve horizontally and sandwich the layers together with half the chocolate buttercream. Place on the board and frost with the remaining chocolate buttercream.

Cover the cake board: Use the red fondant to cover the edges of the board (see page 17).

Baubles: Divide the vanilla buttercream among 3 bowls. Add red food coloring to one bowl, green to the second, and yellow to the third. Frost 3 cupcakes with one color each of the buttercream, doming it up in the center and spreading as smoothly as possible with a metal spatula. Press a halved gummy candy onto one side of each cupcake. Cut ¾-inch (2 cm) pieces of strawberry lace and bend each into a loop. Secure to the gummy candies with red decorator frosting.

Decoration: Decorate the baubles using the tubes of decorator frosting, strawberry lace, candy-coated chocolates, and edible gold balls.

Finishing touches: Carefully peel the paper away from the rectangles of brown fondant and gently press around the sides of the cake to complete the box. Arrange the cupcakes in the chocolate box. Tie the ribbon around the cake and secure in place with decorator frosting.

Templates

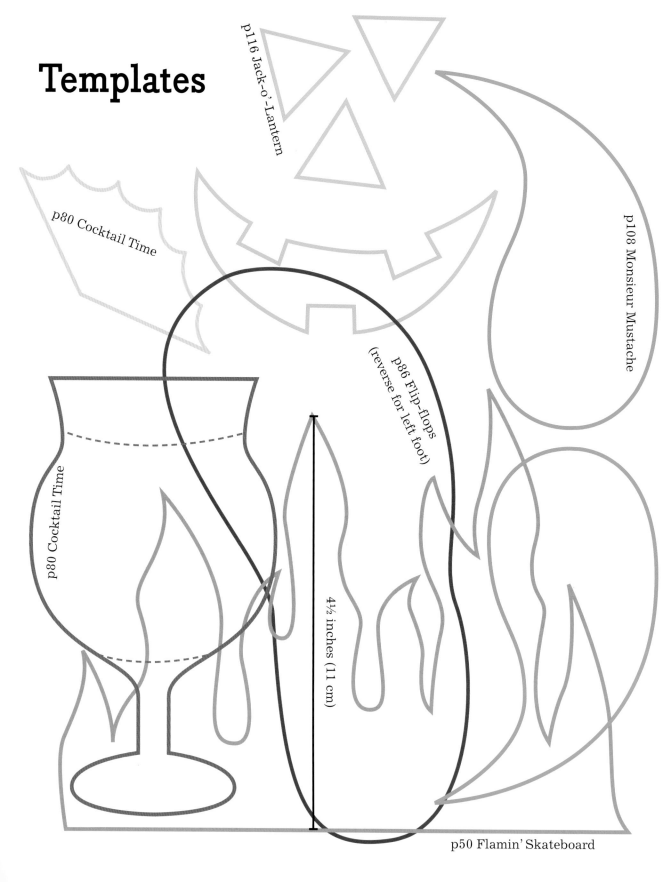

p116 Jack-o'-Lantern

p80 Cocktail Time

p108 Monsieur Mustache

p80 Cocktail Time

p86 Flip-flops
(reverse for left foot)

4½ inches (11 cm)

p50 Flamin' Skateboard

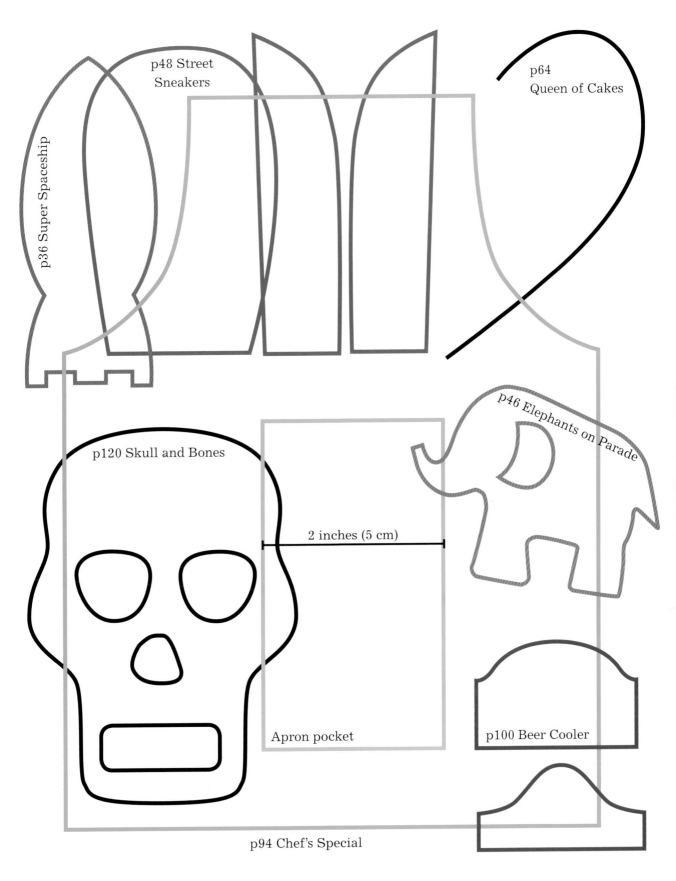

p36 Super Spaceship

p48 Street Sneakers

p64 Queen of Cakes

p46 Elephants on Parade

p120 Skull and Bones

2 inches (5 cm)

Apron pocket

p100 Beer Cooler

p94 Chef's Special

Source List

Internet sources for decorating ingredients and sugarcraft equipment supplies. Many of the companies also have retail locations.

USA

A.C. Moore Arts & Crafts
Online and retail supplier
Tel. 1-888-ACMOORE
www.acmoore.com

Candy Direct, Inc.
Online supplier
745 Design Court, Suite 602
Chula Vista, CA 91911
Tel. 619-216-0116
www.candydirect.com

Global Sugar Art
Online supplier
Tel. 1-800-420-6088
www.globalsugarart.com

Michaels Stores, Inc.
Online and retail supplier
Tel. 1-800-MICHAELS
www.michaels.com

N.Y. Cake & Baking Dist.
Online supplier
56 West 22nd Street
NY, NY 10010
Tel. 212-675-CAKE
www.nycake.com

Pfeil & Holing
Online supplier
Tel. 1-800-247-7955
www.cakedeco.com

Sweet Factory
Online and retail supplier
Tel: 877-817-9338
www.sweetfactory.com

Wilton Industries
Online and retail supplier
Tel. 1-800-794-5866
www.wilton.com

Canada

Michaels Stores, Inc.
Online and retail supplier
Tel. 1-800-MICHAELS
www.michaels.com

UK

Almond Art
Online supplier
Unit 15/16, Faraday Close
Gorse Lane Industrial Estate
Clacton-on-Sea
Essex CO15 4TR
Tel. 01255 223 322
www.almondart.com

Blue Ribbon Sugarcraft Centre
Online and retail supplier
29 Walton Road
East Molesey
Surrey KT8 0DH
Tel. 020 8941 1591
www.blueribbons.co.uk

Jane Asher Party Cakes
Online and retail supplier
22–24 Cale Street
London SW3 3QU
Tel. 020 7584 6177
www.janeasher.com

Squires Kitchen
Online and retail supplier
Squires Kitchen
3 Waverley Lane
Farnham
Surrey GU9 8BB
Tel. 0845 61 71 810
www.squires-shop.com/uk

Australia & New Zealand

Cake Deco
Online and retail supplier
Shop 7, Port Philip Arcade
232 Flinders Street
Melbourne, Victoria
Australia
Tel. 03 9654 5335
www.cakedeco.com.au

Milly's
Online and retail supplier
273 Ponsonby Road
Auckland
New Zealand
Tel. 0800 200 123
www.millyskitchen.co.nz

South Africa

Kadies Bakery Supplies
Online and retail supplier
Kingfisher Shopping Centre
Kingfisher Drive
Fourways
Gauteng
South Africa
Tel. 027 11 465-5572
www.kadies.co.za